ELIZA ASBURY

HER COTTAGE AND HER SON

To George and Martha
God Bless You
David Hallam
Asbury Cottage
England
15 August 2003

Eliza Asbury
Reproduced with permission from the
Methodist Collection of Drew University Library.

ELIZA ASBURY

HER COTTAGE AND HER SON

DAVID J.A. HALLAM

BREWIN BOOKS

First published by
Brewin Books Ltd, 56 Alcester Road,
Studley, Warwickshire B80 7LG in 2003
www.brewinbooks.com

ISBN 1 85858 235 0

A Cataloguing in Publication Record
for this title is available from the British Library.

Front Cover: (top) Portrait of Eliza Asbury; (bottom) Eliza's cottage, Newton, Great Barr.
Back Cover: (top) All Saints, West Bromwich, also known as the Old Church, Bromwich Heath;
(top middle) The Old Forge Mill Farm, Sandwell Valley; (bottom middle) Sandwell Valley Farm;
(bottom) David Hallam (left) with Harry Clarke, curator of the Asbury Cottage Museum.

Typeset in Times
Printed in Great Britain by
Warwick Printing

Contents

*'Preached at Barr, a village famous for nothing as having
given birth to Mr Francis Asbury of America and being the
present residence of his parents, at whose house we preached'*

**Diary of Samuel Taylor
Itinerant Methodist Preacher
11 June 1792** [i]

[i] *PWHS Vol XXII p121 (1939).*

Acknowledgements

This book has been made possible with the help of many people. The published work remains entirely my responsibility and I would like to acknowledge the assistance and encouragement from the following people and institutions.

Staff of Sandwell MBC Museums and Libraries Dept, especially Ruth Holloway and Harry Clarke who have primary responsibility for the care of the cottage. Also Nigel Haynes, Conservation Officer, Sandwell MBC and the staff the local studies archive at Smethwick Library.
Prof John Wigger of the University of Missouri for the supply of much unpublished material, and advice during the course of research.
Peter Forsaith of The Wesley Centre, Oxford Brookes University.
Sunni Johnson and Wanda Hall of the Baltimore Lovely Lane Museum.
Staff of the Methodist Archives, Drew University.
Staff of Stafford County Record Office, City of Birmingham Library Local Studies and Archive Department, the staff of the library at Queen's College, Birmingham.
Dr. Roger Shinton and other colleagues at Birmingham Heartlands Hospital.
Harry Clarke, G Ian Goodson, Maurice Hobbs and John Wigger, who kindly read the first draft and made helpful comments.
To Rev Geof Whitfield and Rev Adedoja Adedimeji.
My children James, Grace and Owen for their forbearance and above all my wife Claire for giving me the space and time to complete the project.

David Hallam

Illustrations

Preface

Much is known of the life of Francis Asbury, the first Bishop of the Methodist Episcopal Church of the United States of America. He introduced methods of evangelism such as camp meetings, Sunday schools and travelling preachers, which set the tone for the whole Evangelical movement.

On Thursday 12 September 1771, eight days out into the Atlantic from the port of Pill near Bristol, England, he began to keep a daily journal. Fortyfour years later, on Thursday 7 December 1815, the pen fell from his hands and he died the following March, 1816.

At his death he was one of the most respected and venerated men in the newly formed United States. Schools, colleges, churches, neighbourhoods, streets and even children were to be named "Asbury" in his honour.

He spent those fortyfour years travelling throughout the colonies, later to become the first states of the USA. He is believed to have preached 16,550 sermons, and ridden over a quarter of a million miles. When he arrived in 1771 there were just 550 Methodists concentrated in New York and Philadelphia. By 1816 there were 250,000 Methodists ministered to by 700 ordained preachers.

By contrast little is known about the life of his parents, Elizabeth and Joseph Asbury. Whilst their son travelled America, they patiently remained in their cottage at Newton, Great Barr, in England.

They lived during a period which was occasionally dangerous for Methodists. At close quarters they saw the world's first industrial revolution. Week in and week out their tiny cottage served as a church. They were certainly not rich, nor particularly well educated.

Eliza Asbury was evidently the major influence on her remarkable son. This Black Country woman now has her portrait hanging at a major American university. Her tiny cottage is a museum to the memory of her son, visited by hundreds of tourists each year, many from the United States.

Dedicated to the memory of
Bob Masters
1926-2000
Hackney and Thanet Councillor,
mentor and friend.

1. Early Years

One of her son's biographers, writing sixty years after her death tells us that "the memory of Mrs Asbury is lovingly cherished by a few old people who knew her personally and by many others to whom her excellencies of character have often been told" [ii]

Elizabeth Asbury, known as Eliza [iii], died at her cottage at Newton near Great Barr in south Staffordshire in January 1802.

Eliza's British born son was seen as one of the founders of the new American republic. He helped shape the way in which countless Americans today express their religious beliefs. John Wesley's mother Susannah is sometimes called "The Mother of Methodism". Eliza Asbury can justifiably be remembered as the "Mother of American Evangelicalism".

Yet her own son was aware that she was, in her early life, very much a "woman of this world". She and Joseph Asbury started married life without a family bible and apparently failed to baptise the son who became the first Methodist bishop.

It would not be unusual for a woman of Eliza's social status to disappear from history. Countless generations came and went in England, with the only record of their lives being a few sketchy details of baptism, marriage and burial in a parish register. Even these meagre records varied from parish to parish and clergyman to clergyman. Many of the details of Eliza Asbury's life have proved elusive to researchers over two centuries.

Much of what we do know comes from Frank's brief notes in his journal [iv] and some surviving letters between the two [v]. Soon after Frank's own death, biographers sought information about his early life and learnt of Eliza's contribution to Methodism.

The cottage in Newton, Great Barr brings Eliza's story to life. It was here that Eliza bought up Frank, lived with her husband Joseph for nearly fifty years and in which they both died. The cottage is now one of the oldest surviving buildings in the West Midlands, one of the few homes of an identified working family from that period. It is also one of the few known venues of the Methodist and non-conformist cottage meetings which had such a profound impact on British life in the second half of the 18th century.

Her son's letters and journal, together with what is known about this fascinating area, make it possible to create a picture of what life would have been like for this woman, never very rich, but immensely loved by all around her.

[ii] *Briggs p9.* [iii] *J&L Vol III p184.* [iv] *J&L Vol I pp 123-125, 720-722 & Vol II 333-334.* [v] *J&L Vol III; letters from Frank p3-8, 13-18, 35-37, 39, 46-47, 85, 121-122, 127-128, 130, 134-135, 137, 142-146, 166-167, 169-171, 181, 182-180, 184-185; from Eliza 184-185.*

The name "Asbury" is associated with the English West Midlands and it is likely that Joseph Asbury, Eliza's husband, came from a family which had lived in the area for many generations. Several Asburys are to be found in the parish records in the parishes of Polesworth, Sheldon, Bickenhill, Elmdon and Tanworth in Arden area of north Warwickshire. It is from this branch of the family that Joseph probably originates. The spelling of the name changes, a Simon Asberie appears in Bickenhill, whilst Frank's sister Sarah's surname is spelt as Ashbury at Handsworth [vi].

We know that Eliza, whose maiden name was Rogers came from a Welsh family, which had probably settled in Birmingham. We know that she had at least one brother Nathaniel and sister, Sarah, both of whom also became Methodists [vii].

Her father may have been the John Rogers, wrongly spelt on that occasion as "Roggers", who had his son John baptised at St. Martins in the Bullring, Birmingham on 3 December 1708. A John Rogers returned on 2 October 1714 to baptise Sarah, and again on the 10 October 1716 to baptise Eliz Rogers [viii], though only conjecture allows us to suggest this may be the registration of Eliza's baptism.

The names of John and Elizabeth Rogers appear again in the Parish Register for St Giles in the village of Sheldon, a few miles to the east of Birmingham, now within the city boundary and close to the airport.

A John Rogers and Mary Wright, both listed as being from the Parish of St Martins in Birmingham, were married at St Giles on 6 December 1741.

Eliza had probably moved to Sheldon with her brother John and new sister in law the previous year, living with them as a "servant or sojourner" a custom for younger sisters. It would not be unusual at that time for men such as John to wait until their 30s to get married, nor was Eliza, then 26, by any means unusual in still being a spinster, with the average age of marriage for women in Warwickshire parishes ranging between 24 and 28 years [ix].

In the following year Joseph Asbury married Elizabeth Rogers, both listed as then being resident in the parish on, 30 May 1742.

A few days later on 3 June another Asbury, Edward, of Elmdon married a Mary Green. Thereafter for several years the Asburys are well represented in the parishes baptismal registers through a Thomas Asbury, who had many children, whilst the marriage remains the only entry for Joseph and Elizabeth [x].

Sheldon like many of the villages in Warwickshire and possibly those in other counties surrounding Birmingham, did not have a stable population, Family names came and went in the parish register over a short period. Sheldon recorded more baptisms than burials, yet its population stayed about the same, with the excess population being exported to Birmingham and other villages [xi].

[vi] *Skipp 1963 p50.* [vii] *J&L Vol III p85.* [viii] *Parish Records for St Martins in the Bullring, Birmingham, held at the Birmingham Public Library.* [ix] *J.M.Martin 1976.* [x] *Parish Records for St Giles, Sheldon, Vol 3 held at Birmingham Public Library, though this particular page is mis filed.* [xi] *Skipp 1960 p28-29.*

Those already in Sheldon had an interest in discouraging settlement, it was a "closed" parish – owning a house gave access to the common grazing land. The more houses, the less grazing land to go round, with those already in the parish keen to be rid of any uninvited stranger [xii].

Within months Eliza was pregnant. Joseph and Elizabeth moved to a new home, and Joseph had a job with the Wyrley Birch family at Hamstead Hall. At first they lived in a cottage close to Hamstead Bridge and Mill, on the Wyrley Birch estate, probably on the site of the present day Walcot Drive.

The baptism of their first child is recorded in the parish register for St Mary's Handsworth: "Sarah daughter of Jas. Eliz Asbury May 3 AD 1743". Frank was apparently born just over two years later, which he believed to have been on the 20 or 21 August 1745 [xiii], though on which day he evidently wasn't certain.

Surprisingly, in view of Frank's later ordination and enthronement as a Bishop there is no record of Franks baptism at St Mary's. He could, of course, have been baptised at another nearby church but it is not recorded in the surrounding parishes of All Saints, West Bromwich, nor at nearby Aston Juxta. If his baptism was delayed by the family move, then it may have been recorded at St Margaret's at Barre as they had crossed the parish boundary, but there is no record there either. Some parents took their children back to the church of their wedding for baptism, but again, there is no record of Frank being baptised at St Giles, Sheldon.

Then: The cottage at Hamstead where Sarah and Frank were born.

Now: The site has long since been redeveloped into a housing estate.

[xii] *Skipp 1963 p38.* [xiii] *J&L Vol I p720.*

This issue has been researched by others. An eminent Methodist historian, Frank Baker, made enquiries and reported "Local enquiries elicit the fact that for some reason he was not baptised, as his elder sister had been in the Parish Church of Handsworth" [xiv].

There is no evidence at that time that either Elizabeth or Joseph were refusing to baptise Frank on grounds of religious objection, as did some of the dissenters, Quakers or Presbyterians This failure to baptise Frank could well reflect their entire lack of interest in religion or faith which characterised Eliza in the early years of Frank's life.

As we shall see Eliza and Joseph were not particularly religious at the time of Frank's birth or even for much of his childhood, referring to himself as having been bought up in an "ungodly family" [xv].

In 1795, when fifty years old, Frank wrote and asked his parents to check the church register so that he would know the exact date [xvi]. To which he received, from Eliza, an apparently evasive reply [xvii].

Shortly after Frank's birth, the Asbury's with their two children moved about a mile and a half to a relatively new terrace of brick built artisans' cottages, probably roofed with inexpensive brown clay tiles. It was at right angles to the rear of the Malt Shovel public house and brewery in the hamlet of Newton, Great Barr, to which it may have been 'tied' by employment.

The cottage had two rooms on the ground floor, with two bedrooms upstairs. Under the stairs there was a half cellar which may have been used for storage. In the larger room downstairs was an inglenook fireplace, which provided a main hearth for warmth, hot water and some cooking space.

The cottage windows probably didn't have glass but would have had shuttering which would have been opened and closed during the course of the day. Nor would the chimney stack been surmounted by a chimney pot.

Close to the house were some barns in which, during later years, Frank would play and later the Methodists meet.

A neighbour, Widow Bromwich, was evicted from her slightly bigger house in 1749 for non-payment of rent to the Gough family, one of the local landowners. Her goods, worth £19.6s9d (about $15 US) were seized and the inventory gives some idea of what would be in a typical house.

In the kitchen Widow Bromwich had various pewter tankards, a dripping pan, a large and a small iron spit, a fire shovel, a salt box, pewter plates, a tin colander, a clock, a dresser, several chairs and a long table.

The parlour, or living room, had sixteen chairs and a small oval table. Each of the three bedrooms had a bedstead, feather mattress, bolsters, pillows, a little table and a chest. She also had a cellar with a half hogshead of beer, her own brew house with

[xiv] *Methodist Recorder, August 16, 1945.* [xv] *J&L Vol I p125.* [xvi] *J&L Vol III p135.* [xvii] *J&L Vol III p184. Parish records and Bishops transcript for St. Marys Handsworth held at Birmingham Public Library.*

Then: The Asbury cottage, far end of terrace.   *Now: The Cottage today.*

The sitting room.   *The Inglenook fireplace.*

The master bedroom where Eliza slept.   *The small bedroom which Frank occupied.*

various tubs and a stable empty except for a wheel barrow, a collar and harness and a pot of iron cleaner.

The most valuable single item was the clock which was said to be worth £1.8s6d. The long table in the kitchen had immediately been bought by a Mr Gibbon for 7s, though he hadn't then paid for it when the inventory had been drawn up.

The house had just two candlesticks and presumably like the Asburys, Widow Bromwich and her family would make the best use of natural light or that from the fire [xviii].

The Widow Bromwich inventory refers to a "brewhouse". This was a separate or attached smaller building where much of the cooking and other household work would be undertaken. The cottage at Newton probably had a similar arrangement, though this has now been demolished.

Water would be supplied from a nearby well or spring, possibly shared with other families.

Sanitation would probably be through an earth closet. This was a hole in the ground, over which was a plank for sitting, with a round hole through which they would pass their waste. Each morning the "night soil" from chambers pots, the "guzunder", would be poured into the closet followed by ashes from the cottage grate. From time to time the hole would be cleaned and dug out. This would be in a shelter a few yards from the house, though the site has not yet been subject to an archaeological survey [xix].

We know that at some point Eliza had acquired enough education to be able to read. Frank recalls coming home each afternoon to find her reading a Bible using the light from the west facing ground floor window.

Frank also notes in later life that although she had the skill to read, she didn't have the skill to write. Whether this was due to incapacity – though there is no evidence of blindness – or incomplete education we cannot be certain.

The picture which emerges of Joseph and Eliza Asbury is that both knew the value of skills and education. In their lifetime they were to see the old rural certainties go.

What were villages, even small hamlets, in their childhood – Wednesbury, Handsworth, Bromwich Heath, Smethwick, Oldbury, Aston – had become overcrowded towns by their thirties.

The Asburys would have seen thousands of men and women without skills, education, capital or land migrating to the area, with possibly Eliza or her family among their ranks. There were many casualties.

That clearly wasn't what the Joseph and Eliza Asbury's wanted for their children and they probably determined at an early age that both would be given at least a very basic education.

[xviii] *Inventory of Widow Bromwich 1749, Gough Archives, Birmingham Public Library.* [xix] *Conversation with Nigel Haynes, Sandwell MBC Conservation Officer, Jan 2003.*

A regular job in a changing world for the bread winner, a new home, a beautiful daughter and a lively toddler boy.

Frank later recalled that they were people "in common life; were remarkable for honesty and industry, and had all things needed to enjoy ; had my father been as saving as laborious, he might have been wealthy

But within months of moving to the new home a tragedy was to overcome the Asburys and destroy their idyllic home together. What happened was probably retold by Eliza many times as a testimony in Frank's hearing, and eventually recorded in his Journal.

2. Crisis and Conversion

Many families in 18th century England kept a family Bible. Inside would be recorded the births, death and marriages. By writing to his parents requesting that they check his exact date of birth in the parish records, Frank was revealing that Joseph and Elizabeth did not keep a family Bible. Eliza at the time was, according to her son, very much a woman of the world.

The beloved Sarah, their only daughter, then just coming up for her fifth birthday, fell ill, died and was buried at St Mary's Handsworth on 28 May 1748. Frank would have been about two years and nine months old.

This was a turning point for Eliza. The death of her only daughter in her early thirties destroyed Eliza emotionally and she suffered a profound breakdown. The knowledge that Frank had not been baptised may have added to her grief.

Frank Asbury recalled that Sarah was his mother's favourite, "My dear mother being very affectionate, sank into deep distress at the loss of a darling child from which she was not relieved for many years."

This must have been difficult for the growing Frank. About those years of psychological collapse he recorded "how would the bereaved mother weep and tell of the beauties and excellencies of her lost and lovely child! Pondering on the past in the silent suffering of hopeless grief."

Eliza Asbury was living "in a very, dark, dark, dark day and place". She saw herself "a lost and wretched sinner" with few people around who were able and willing to help her. She apparently sought help from local clergy. Many religious people she found, however, were "in the times of this ignorance", few were "sound in the faith" or "faithful to the grace given."

Real help apparently came in the form of a renewed Christian faith probably encouraged by evangelistic Methodists or Baptists. "Under the dispensation" of this breakdown, "God was pleased to open her eyes" explained Frank.

St Mary's, Handsworth.

Eliza began to "read almost constantly when leisure presented the opportunity". She spent days in reading and prayer. Eventually she understood: "she found justifying grace, and pardoning mercy."

In a very short space of time, the cottage at Barr changed dramatically. Eliza encouraged her husband and surviving child to family Bible reading and prayer with the singing of Psalms and no doubt many of the new hymns written by Charles Wesley.

Frank was well aware of the impact upon his life "I was a moral youth and remarkably fond of reading the Holy Scripture from a boy" he was to tell his companion John Wesley Bond shortly before his death in 1816, "which by the particular attention of my mother I was able to do distinctly at the age of five" [xx].

Eliza may have found keeping her faith difficult, perhaps on occasions "back-sliding". One of her son's biographers quotes a letter from Frank when he referred to his midnight walks for prayer and wanted "to hide appearances from my poor ungodly yet otherwise kind mother" [xxi].

Eliza's assurance of divine grace was not without a cost. Frank records how "Sometimes I was much ridiculed, and called "Methodist Parson", because my mother invited any people who had the appearance of religion to her house" [xxii].

Eliza's renewed faith would have become apparent just a few years after the ferocious anti-Methodist riots centred on Wednesbury just three miles to the west. These started on 20 May 1743 and continued for six months. The riots broke out again in January 1744 and continued into March.

Houses were smashed and burnt, Methodist women were assaulted and worse [xxiii], men were held over coal pits, and property stolen. The mobs fanned out all over the surrounding countryside – Darlaston, West Bromwich, Tipton, Birmingham, Walsall, and Aldridge [xxiv].

Violence and the persecution of Methodists by mobs and local constables continued sporadically into 1747 when a preacher named Joseph Cownley was attacked in Darlaston, Wednesbury and Walsall and the local societies were charged with "superstition".

Eliza would have been well aware of the dangers she faced as a Methodist. She by then had relatives in Wednesbury. Her husband's employer at Hamstead Hall, John Wyrley Birch, as a "resolute magistrate" was to play an important part in curtailing the persecution in Birmingham [xxv].

Near neighbours of the Asburys at Great Barr, Robert Ault and his wife, had moved from Aldridge, because their house had been destroyed in 1745. Their son Thomas became a lifelong friend of Frank [xxvi].

[xx] *Bond, John Wesley p24.* [xxi] *WL Duren, ref to unpublished MS.* [xxii] *J&L Vol I p720.* [xxiii] *WJ Wilkinson says "The wife of Joshua Constable was abused by the mob as she was on her way to Wednesbury in a manner too shocking to relate" p87. An account of the incident sent to John Wesley and quoted by AC Pratt Black Country Methodism, London 1891, Kelly says "five or six held her down, that another might force her. But she continued to resist, till they changed their purpose, beat her much, and went away." p147.* [xxiv] *Hackwood "West Bromwich" 1895 p209-214.* [xxv] *PWHS Vol 11 p99 (1919).* [xxvi] *Hackwood "West Bromwich" 1895 p227.*

As late as 1787 Edward Hand, another friend of the Asburys, was evicted for his religious activities from his home in Hill Hook near where Sutton Coldfield's Blake Street railway station now stands. His furniture was turned out onto the lane together with his family. It was reported that "...amidst the tumult and distress of the moment, Hand's daughter, Tamar, was seen kneeling in the midst of the crowd praying for their persecutors" [xxvii].

This persecution took place in a context where the brutalities and opportunities of industrialisation were apparent for all to see. Between 1700 and 1800 the population of Britain doubled, much of that growth was in Birmingham and the Black Country.

Georgian Britain "...was a violent society in which savage crimes such as murder and rape were common... highway robbery was a common resort for the desperate poor; all classes engaged gleefully in brutal sports from bear baiting and cock fighting to bare knuckle boxing... Gambling was a near universal mania... Alcohol was consumed on a gargantuan scale; cheap gin devastated lives... sexual promiscuity was a male privilege... venereal disease was rampant in all groups of society" [xxviii]

All around them the Asburys would see new forges, new mines, new furnaces, new shanty towns, new factories and new threats. It was neither an easy place or time to live, especially for a Methodist.

Cock fighting as depicted in Hogarth's painting 'Cockpit Royal'.

John Wesley preaching at the Market Cross.

xxvii W.C. Sheldon p9. *xxviii* Michael St John Parker, p24.

Methodism was a major component of an evangelical movement which was challenging both the established church and the new economic order. John Wesley and his preachers proclaimed a simple four fold message:

All need to be saved (original sin);
All can be saved (universal salvation);
All can know they are saved (assurance)
All can be saved to the uttermost (Christian perfection) [xxix]

Eliza's conversion was classic. She clearly felt that she needed salvation and accepted the assurance promoted by the Wesleyan movement. In her bereaved world which seemed dark, with a detached husband and an unstable neighbourhood, Methodism offered her an anchor, a lifeline.

[xxix] *Stacey, p268.*

3. The Industrious Husband

Joseph Asbury was a very different person from his wife, Eliza. We have no contemporary record of brothers, sisters or his parents, though he almost certainly had relations in the area. The Thomas and Edward Asbury whose marriages were registered at Sheldon may have been his brothers.

Joseph's job as a gardener at Hamstead Hall would have required some skill. The gardens of the big houses in Georgian England provided fruit, vegetables and floral decorations for the entire household throughout the year. With careful planning and continuous tending, seasonal plants would have their growth brought forward or retarded.

A similar garden to that at Hamstead Hall can be found at Sandwell Park Farm, just a mile or so further up the Tame Valley. It provided the kitchen garden for the Earl of Dartmouth's Sandwell Valley estate and is now open to the public.

In addition to his work as a gardener at for the Wyrley Birches at Hamstead Hall, he had a second job. He may have been employed as a farmer, or at the nearby malt house, possibly for the Gough estate, though there is no evidence for this. Frank says his father worked for two of richest families in the area and the Goughs were among the richest, together with the Scots and Dartmouths.

When describing his mother's breakdown Frank doesn't mention his father's reaction to the death of Sarah, or even Joseph's response to his wife's distress. The only reference Frank makes to Joseph expressing any sort of emotion was at the time of his departure for America in 1771 [xxx].

Sandwell Valley Farm, similar to the farm at Hamstead Hall where Joseph worked.

[xxx] *J&L Vol II p162.*

It is clear that Joseph supported both Eliza and Frank in their Methodist work by providing hospitality, allowing Eliza to hold meetings in the home and the barn and being generous to the cause.

There is however no evidence that Joseph found the same assurance of faith which inspired his wife and son. Frank's makes this clear in his journal and letters. After receiving her assurance Frank recalls "I well remember my mother strongly urged my father to family reading and prayer…" xxxi.

It may be that Joseph supported Eliza because he had seen for himself the enormous change which had overtaken her, when she had received assurance. Eliza must have been difficult to live with when going through her breakdown.

Joseph Asbury was not happy with his son's decision to go to America. Losing his only child may have been a step too far. As Frank left Great Barr his father realised the enormity of what was happening and shouted "I shall never see him again".

Many, many times Frank enquired in his letters home about his father's spiritual condition. At first he addressed the enquiry to both parents, but as time wore on Frank concentrated on his father's spiritual welfare.

It is clear that Frank feared they would be separated in the afterlife "Does my father give his heart to God? Has he victory over sin more than ever? Is his soul devoted to God? It is a trial for us to be parted; but whatever will it be for us to be eternally parted?" xxxii.

Later he implores "My dear Father, cry to God for grace to conquer sin. Take abundantly more care of your soul than your body. I pray for, think of, Oh that I could weep over, you more. May God restore you to his favour, and image and glory" xxxiii. He goes on to ask them to "Live in love together". It was not only Frank who feared for Joseph's soul. John Allen, another preacher who wrote to Eliza in 1772, also made reference to Joseph's lack of commitment.

Frank referred to his father as being "remarkable for honesty and industry…had my father been as saving as laborious, he might have been wealthy" xxxiv.

In one letter dated 1784 Frank refers to the possibility of his mother and father emigrating to America to be with him.

One of the reasons why Frank discounts the idea is that there would be difficulty employing his father: "I have one friend," he said, "a great man who would maybe employ my father in the way he would choose, but it is too much like Hamstead Hall" xxxv.

Now this statement begs many questions. On the one hand Frank tells us his father was honest and industrious, on the other hand he fears that employment in America would bring up some undisclosed problems which were obvious in his employment at Hamstead Hall with the Wyrley Birches.

xxxi Ibid. xxxii J&L Vol III p17. xxxiii J&L Vol III p37. xxxiv J&L Vol I p720. xxxv J & L Vol III p36.

The conclusion that we may draw is that Joseph's problems went beyond a refusal to accept the gospel as proclaimed by eighteenth century Methodism. There was some other problem which ensnared him, cost him a great deal, and caused problems in his work. This was possibly drink, or gambling, or both.

Joseph and Eliza lived in a tied cottage, probably attached to a farm, linked to the malt house and Malt Shovel pub. Frank referred to his father as being employed as a farmer and a gardener, possibly Joseph ran the farm growing, harvesting and storing, the barley used in beer production. Labourers were often paid in "truck" – payment in kind. If Joseph did have a drink problem, supply would have been no problem.

Late in life Joseph may have attempted to reform. Frank had been told of this change but challenged "I hope the accounts I have had of the piety of you both are not too large" [xxxvi].

An account of Joseph's death in 1798 gives us a clue. Frank records in his Journal that he had received a letter from a friend, Mr Phillips of Birmingham. Phillips is directly quoted as saying "He kept his room six weeks previous to his death; the first month of the time he ate nothing but a little biscuit, and the last fortnight he took nothing but a little spirits and water – he died very happy" [xxxvii].

The extract from Phillip's letter in the Journal amounted to just 40 words, Frank made no comment. Four years later, when Frank heard the news of his mother's death he put an obituary in his journal of 421 words, one of his longer entries.

Joseph Asbury, however, has become a figure of some controversy. There has been a belief among some American Asburys that Eliza Rodgers was in fact Joseph Asbury's second wife. Many Asburys, including Mrs Elisabeth Dole a US senator and wife of a former Presidential candidate, are believed to be blood relations with Frank on the basis of descent from a child of this first marriage.

Herbert Asbury a celebrated writer, whose other works included "The Gangs of New York" which was made into a film in 2002, published a bitter account of Frank Asbury's life entitled "A Methodist Saint – The Life of Bishop Asbury". Herbert had been bought up among Methodists in America's Deep South and believed them to be hypocrites.

His book on Frank starts with a "family legend" that when pregnant with Frank, God appeared to Eliza and told her that her son would be a great religious leader. This story has not been recounted anywhere else.

Herbert Asbury claimed that Joseph Asbury had first married a Susan Whipple, the daughter of a farmer from Wednesbury. Susan had died shortly after giving birth to a boy named Thomas, who was then bought up by relatives.

Herbert believed that Thomas ran away to sea, got into trouble and was disowned by Joseph, who, Herbert tells us, refused to have anymore to do with Thomas, believing him to be an "infidel".

xxxvi J&L Vol III p145. xxxvii J&L Vol II p163.

Thomas settled in Fairfax County, Virginia and one of his sons, Daniel, became a Methodist preacher in North Carolina. He was the great grandfather of Herbert Asbury.

In later years Frank Asbury made several references in his Journal to meeting both a Daniel and Thomas Asbury in America but there is no suggestion of a blood relationship with either. Later editors of the journal say in their explanatory notes that Thomas came from a north Staffordshire branch of the family. The Herbert Asbury story is also disputed on the very first page of the 1958 edition of Asbury's Journal and Letters.

The author has conducted an exhaustive search for the name Whipple in contemporary parish archives for Wednesbury and the surrounding area of south Staffordshire, and north Warwickshire, where the Asbury name is well represented in parish records. Later business directories and census records have also been examined

There is no evidence available to suggest that a family named Whipple ever lived in or around Wednesbury, or anywhere else in the West Midlands. Even if it were not possible to find the actual marriage registration between Joseph Asbury and Susan Whipple, the Whipples would have left some other trace. The father, mother, brothers, sisters and cousins of Susan Whipple would have been married, baptised, buried, but there are no records of this family name.

A so-called "genealogical study" was presented by a branch of the Asbury family to the Lovely Lane Methodist Museum Baltimore in 1964. It provides no evidence to support the story and is not based on any original research.

A variation of this story, told to the author by a relative of Herbert Asbury, is that Joseph had been born in America and had re-emigrated to England, marrying in Polesworth, north Warwickshire, shortly after his sixteenth birthday in 1731.

A Joseph Asbury is to be found in the Polesworth parish register, and he did have a son called Thomas. But other entries point to a different story. This Joseph Asbury had married Sarah Baxter in May 1724. They had a child, John, born a month later, another child Joseph came in 1725, a daughter Eleonor in 1728 who lived just two years. They had a son Thomas in 1731.

Two years later, in 1734, Joseph and Sarah had another daughter who they again called Eleonor. Tragically this Joseph Asbury was to die in March 1734 leaving a widow and four children.

Whatever the truth of this story we can be without doubt that Eliza was the spiritual and emotional rock upon which Frank was able to build his faith and resolve. It was with her that he had the animated discussions about religion. She encouraged him to go to a Methodist meeting. It was Eliza that local people remembered for many years after her death.

4. *"A Darke Place called Great Barre"*

On hearing of his mother's death Frank writes "For fifty years her hands, her house, her heart were open to receive the people of God and the ministers of Christ; and thus a lamp was lighted up in a dark place called Great Barre in Great Britain" [xxxviii].

A letter to his cousin a few months later reiterated his belief that Great Barr was "the dark place of my nativity" [xxxix].

Today Great Barr is chiefly remembered for what happened in the grand house of Great Barr Hall. From 1765 onwards it was one of the venues of the monthly meetings of the Lunar Society, which were carefully fixed to coincide with the full moon to enable its members to safely cross Hamstead and Handsworth back to Birmingham or their country houses [xl].

The Lunar Society included Matthew Boulton, James Watt, Joseph Priestley, Erasmus Darwin, William Murdoch and Josiah Wedgwood [xli]. These were the people who controlled and shaped the industry and science of the newly emerging West Midlands, though it is doubtful if any members of the Asbury family were even aware of the society's existence until the terrible riots of 1791 when the Lunar Society held a dinner in Birmingham to celebrate the French Revolution.

But why did Frank see Great Barr as being "a darke place"?

There's little doubt that he didn't always get on with the other children of the parish. Nor did he have a high opinion of the local church, St. Margaret's, referring to their lack of help during his mother's breakdown and rejecting the local clergyman as a "blind priest" Nor did he care much for his first employers, where he lived in one of the "wealthiest and most ungodly families in the parish" [xlii].

After his mother's death Frank wrote to local Methodists enquiring after the society at Barr and saying "I should like to subscribe something annually to keep the lamp burning", obviously convinced that Great Barr was still in darkness.

However it is difficult to see from Frank's description why Great Barr was a particularly "Dark" place. Indeed the evidence from nineteenth century biographers, taken at face value, suggests a settled country parish. One of his earliest Methodist friends Thomas Ault grew up in the same hamlet and presumably was a childhood playmate. So what happened?

Since the expansion of Birmingham in the mid-twentieth century Great Barr has been a comparatively respectable suburb which straddles the area of three Metropolitan councils – the City of Birmingham, Sandwell and Walsall.

xxxviii J&L Vol II p333. xxxix J&L Vol II p243. xl Hackwood "Handsworth" 2001 p127. xli "The Lunar Society" 2nd part of "Matthew Boulton of Birmingham" published by the City of Birmingham Museum and Art Gallery. Reprint. xlii J&L Vol I p720 - 721.

Great Barr has always been on the boundary lines between the surrounding areas. The Asbury's cottage was just yards from the three way parish boundary between All Saints West Bromwich, St Margaret's Great Barr, and St Mary's Handsworth. The very name Great Barr has been variously applied to Pheasey, parts of Sutton Coldfield, the Newton district of West Bromwich, where the Asburys lived, Booth's Farm, Kingstanding and parts of Walsall.

Great Barr also represented the meeting point of the estates of four great landowning families – the Wyrley Birches and Dartmouths to the south east and south west, with the Scotts to the north and Goughs to the east.

Great Barr was a series of tiny hamlets scattered over the area. Even as late as 1817 it had just 120 recorded houses occupied by 127 families, 78 of whom were engaged in agriculture and 30 in trade, manufacturing or handicrafts [xliii]. There were as many as eleven small hamlets – around the Gough's Arms Inn (later called the Beacon Inn), Howell's Row, Sneal's Green, the West Bromwich Road – that is Newton where the Asbury's lived, Margaret's Lane, Queslett, the Common, Hardwick, Bourn Pool, Bourn Vale, the Tamworth Road, and around Barr Hall.

Those listed as living and working in Newton, just thirty years after Elizabeth Asbury's death, included a tailor, a merchant, a wheelwright, a butcher, a grocer – who doubled as a constable, and a single woman. Newton also had a boarding house and a separate public house, The Malt Shovel. Nearby in other hamlets were a shoemaker, two brickmakers, a thrashing machine owner, a junior gardener, a gun lock maker, three blacksmiths, thirty farmers, one of whom was also a maltser, and four spectacle frame makers [xliv].

Birmingham's first historian, William Hutton however gives a graphic account of what he saw as he first journeyed across the country between Walsall and Birmingham, passing through Barr in 1741.

"I was surprised at the prodigious number of blacksmith's shops upon the road and could not conceive how a country, though populous, could support so many people of the same occupation," say Hutton.

"In some of these shops I observed one, or more, females, stripped of their upper garments, and not overcharged with the lower, wielding the hammer with all the grace of their sex.

"The beauties of their face were rather eclipsed by the smut of the anvil, or, in poetical phrase, the tincture of the forge had taken possession of those lips, which might have been taken by the kiss.

"A fire without heat, a nailer of a fair complexion, or one who despises the tankard, are equally rare among them. His whole system of faith may be comprised in one article

[xliii] Woodall p7. [xliv] White p199 - 200.

– that the slender two penny mug, used in a public house, is deceitful above all things and desperately wicked.

"While the master reaps the harvest of plenty, the workman submits to the scanty gleanings of penury, a thin habit, an early old age, and a figure bending towards the earth. Plenty comes not near his dwelling, except of rags and of children. But few recruits arise from his nail-shop, except for the army. His hammer is worn into deep hollows, fitting the fingers of a dark and plump hand, hard as the timbers it wears. His face, like the moon, is often seen through a cloud" [xlv].

But it wasn't just those who lived in Barr, particularly in Newton that made it "Dark". It was what happened there, day in, day out, throughout the early years of the Midlands industrial revolution, especially as coal and iron production increased to record levels and before the first canal was cut between Wednesbury and Birmingham in 1769. These are the very years, 1750 to 1770, that Asbury would have lived in or visited the hamlet before leaving for America.

Newton was on one of the many drovers' routes between the iron and coalfields of Wednesbury, Darlaston and Walsall and the mills along the River Tame which fed the Birmingham metal trades. This relationship between Aston and Wednesbury had lasted for many years and was a crucial factor in making the West Midlands a major industrial power.

There was a local tradition that the Holloway in Wednesbury was cut between Wednesbury Bridge and Hill Top to enable the drovers to get onto the tracks which led to Aston [xlvi].

Even though the area has now been heavily urbanised it is possible to follow a drovers' trail on a modern street map as it goes down hill from Wednesbury and Stone Cross, across Bromwich Heath, though the Sandwell Valley and then follows the banks of the Tame to Aston: With the exception of Holloway and one or two other stretches the clue is to look for irregular streets with the word "Lane" in their titles:

Holloway - Witton Lane - Jowett's Lane - Clarkes Lane - Heath Lane - Holleyhedge Road - Pennyhill Lane -Water Lane-Wigmore Lane-Ray Hall Lane - Hamstead Road onto the Old Walsall Road - along Rocky Lane to the mills at Perry Barr – or across Hamstead Bridge over the River Tame and into Handsworth [xlvii].

The drovers' trains were huge, especially in the years immediately before the opening of the canal. The demand was such that the comparatively short journey between Wednesbury or Walsall and Birmingham would increase the pithead value for coal of 2 shillings a ton to 10 shillings or more when it was delivered to Birmingham. Packhorse trains, thirty or forty strong, with each horse carrying a hundred-weight, would be headed by the carrier on his horse, ringing a bell to give warning of his approach [xlviii].

[xlv] *Hutton p84-85.* [xlvi] *Ede.* [xlvii] *Birmingham A-Z, Geographers, London 1995 p44-47.* [xlviii] *Ede Ibid p117 quoting Nef The Rise of the British Coal Industry 1 381,383.*

The Malt Shovel Public House, just a few yards from the Asbury cottage would be a natural stopping place for the drovers, especially as they made their return journey and before they started the upward climb to Wednesbury or to Walsall via Stone Cross.

At that time, according to a local historian, Wednesbury, "was less known for its industries as for its pastimes. It was the acknowledged stronghold of the national sport of 'cocking'. Other sports, bull baiting, bear baiting, badger drawing, horse racing, prize fighting and dogfighting were popular, with the "fraternity degenerated into the mere rabble of mobocracy."

A painting by Edward Lewis depicting the Last Bull Bait in 1845.

The popularity of cock fighting in Wednesbury was epitomised by the choice of a golden fighting cock in the design of the lectern in the parish church – believed to be unique.

A local street song described how a cockfighting match between Wednesbury and Walsall turned into a riot. The final verse says:

"Some people may think this strange
Who Wedgebury (Wednesbury) never knew,
But those who have ever been there
Won't have the least doubt it is true
For they are all savage by nature,
And guilty of deeds most shocking-
Jack Baker whacked his own father,
And so ended Wedgebury cocking".

Like all English industrialised towns in the eighteenth century Wednesbury had a huge drink problem [xlix]. The anti Methodist riots of 1743 – 44 and the hunger riots of 1766, showed how easily law and order could break down.

But it wasn't only to drovers that the tiny hamlet of Newton appeared to be a magnet. Each week, just a few hundred years away, where the Scott Arms pub now stands, was a cattle market attracting large crowds [l].

And then there was the growing industrialised town of Birmingham.

[xlix] *Ede p153-156.* [l] *Woodall p24.*

Like Wednesbury, working and living conditions in Birmingham were horrendous. There was massive immigration into the area. In 1720 Birmingham had a population of 11,400. By 1750 it had more than doubled to 23,688, by 1778 it was approaching 42,250 [li].

Overall the three counties which interlock to form the Birmingham and Black Country conurbation saw their population double during the eighteenth century [lii]. Much of that growth was concentrated in towns such as Wednesbury, Darlaston, Tipton, Bilston, West Bromwich and Willenhall, all which had grown from comparatively small villages to have a combined population of nearly 28,000 by 1801 [liii].

These huge populations would spill out into the surrounding countryside for fresh air, rest and recreation. The weekly holiday of "St Monday" would be an occasion for cock fighting, bull baiting, drinking and "gypsy days" to surrounding villages [liv].

The villages which made up Great Barr had several pubs which were used as such resorts, with local people eventually having to set up their own "Association for the Prosecution of Felons" to maintain law and order [lv].

Newton and the wider area of Great Barr was no quiet country backwater. The mills on the River Tame were pushing contemporary technology to its limits. Little more than three miles away Matthew Boulton and his colleagues were planning the world's first factory.

The Asbury's would have seen hundreds of people making their way through the hamlets – immigrants looking for a new life, revellers from the surrounding towns, drovers picking their way between the towns, farmers selling stock at the Scott Arms cattle market, cockfighters enjoying a day of sport and drink.

The Malt Shovel would be a noisy wayside stop, with beer flowing, gambling, cruel sports and much more. The small services, held in the tiny cottage with its Godly congregation, would be a sharp contrast.

[li] *Hopkins.* [lii] *Court p20.* [liii] *Ede, bid Appendix 1 p413.* [liv] *Hopkins p110-111.*
[lv] *Woodall p23, 16.*

5. Educating Her Son

Eliza Asbury was keen that her son had an education, in this she was supported by her husband. It isn't clear whether her aspirations proceeded or followed her religious conversion, but Frank remembers his mother reading her Bible when he was still quite young.

Frank wrote "I was sent to school early, and began to read the Bible between six and seven years of age, and greatly delighted in the historical part of it. My schoolmaster was a great churl, and used to beat me cruelly; this drove me to prayer, and it appeared to me, that God was near me.

"My father having but one son greatly desired to keep me at school, he cared not how long; but in this design he was disappointed; for my master, by his severity had filled me with such horrible dread, that with me anything was preferable to going to school" [lvi].

The school at Snail's Green, another small hamlet in the Great Barr parish about a quarter of a mile north of the cottage, had been endowed in the will of Thomas Addyes in 1722. He had put aside buildings for the school together with land to rent sufficient to pay a schoolmaster to "instruct 13 poor children to read English well, and to write – such children to be nominated from time to time by his brothers, and the heir and survivor of them…"

A nineteenth century report on the school said "The schoolmaster receives the whole of the rents of the land, and the profits of it, and for this educates 20 poor boys of the parish – the number 13, prescribed by the founder, having been increased to 20 many years ago by the trustee, as they thought the improvement in funds sufficient to maintain the increased number. The master makes a quarterly return of the children in the school and the candidates for vacancies, which are filled up as they occur from that list".

"The scholars are taught reading, writing and arithmetic; they find their own books and writing materials and pay 1s a year for firing (heating). In every other respects the instruction is perfectly gratuitous" [lvii].

By the early 1800s a second cousin of Frank's on his mother's side had married the then schoolmaster, Mr Moseley, and a painting of Frank was displayed in the schoolmasters home.

Frank wrote of his childhood "..I abhorred mischief and wickedness, although my mates were amongst the vilest of the vile for lying, swearing, fighting, and whatever

[lvi] *J&L Vol I p720-721.* [lvii] *G. Griffith.*

else boys of their age and evil habits were likely to be guilty of…Sometimes I was much ridiculed and called "Methodist Parson", because my mother invited any people who had the appearance of religion into her home." [lviii].

At first Frank did not know what this meant "but thought it must mean something very bad as it was given me as a nickname, out of reprisal and had as leave they had called me a horse thief." [lix].

Part of Frank's discomfort at the school may have been caused by his mother's choice of dress. He wore a white smock frock and the other lads in derision called him the parson, he also wore a cap like those worn by the children at the Blue Schools in Walsall and Birmingham. Many years later when Bishop, Frank was to refer to "my own colour, light blue" [lx].

Apparently Frank's individuality of dress continued for much of his life. He wore a blue coat when most clergy wore black. By 1810 he was still wearing knee buckles and gaiters, rejecting the new-style pantaloons by then worn by most preachers [lxi].

Elizabeth and Joseph may have been disappointed that their son had not gone on to any further education, if indeed that was possible. His first attempt at employment, in service to one of the most prominent families in the parish ended badly. He then went on to become an apprentice to a family which treated him as their own [lxii].

After that, Frank was one of the many people of that period who benefited from the system of adult education created by the Methodist and Evangelical movement.

Some of it was informal, John Ryland a Church of England curate from Sutton Coldfield, later a leader of the "Church Methodists" in Birmingham with Evangelical sympathies paid Frank several visits, lent him books, walked with him in the lanes and gave him Christian advice. Frank also refers to a travelling shoemaker, a Baptist, who held meetings in the neighbourhood and was invited by Eliza to hold meetings at the cottage [lxiii].

Frank described this encounter "..God sent a pious man, not a Methodist, into our neighbourhood, and my mother invited him to our house; by his conversation and prayers, I was awakened before my fourteenth birthday.

"It was now easy and pleasing to leave my company, and I began to pray morning and evening, being drawn by the cords of love, as with the bands of a man.

The Earl of Dartmouth and Edward Stillingfleet were able to attract some of the top preachers and teachers of the day to the All Saints Church at Bromwich Heath. In some respects it became a centre for the growing Evangelical and Methodist party within the church of England.

It was typical of churches with an Evangelical clergyman in having much more activity than other non-Evangelical churches – as well as formal services, there would

---

[lviii] *J&L Vol II p720.* [lix] *Bond, John Wesley, Anecdotes of Bishop Asbury handwritten MS 1817.* [lx] *J&L Vol III p206.* [lxi] *Wigger p174.* [lxii] *Manuscript of Joseph Reeves dated 1834 MWHS Vol 1 (1965)* [lxiii] *Bond, John Wesley op cit p24.*

have been Bible classes, afternoon readings and lectures [lxiv]. Frank almost had a theological college on his doorstep.

Frank remembers, one suspects with awe, "I soon left our blind priest (at St Margaret's) and went to West Bromwich church: here I heard Ryland, Stillingfleet, Talbot, Bagnall, Mansfield, Hawes and Venn – great names and esteemed Gospel ministers. I became very serious; reading a great deal – Whitfield and Cennick's Sermons and every good book I could meet with" [lxv].

William Hawes.

Edward Stillingfleet was one of the most important Evangelical influences in the Midlands, some believe that he had more influence over Frank Asbury than almost anyone else, acting as mentor, spiritual guide and teacher.

John Mansfield was noted by John Fletcher as a leading Evangelical clergy of the day. William Talbot was vicar of Kineton in south Warwickshire and had been heavily influenced himself by Samuel Walker of Truro one of the earliest Evangelicals who had pioneered bible classes and "Parsons Clubs [lxvi].

During the period that Frank heard him at All Saints, Henry Venn, the Vicar of Huddersfield, would have been working on his book "The Complete Duty of Man" which after publication in 1763 became the classic exposition of Evangelical faith and practice [lxvii].

Henry Venn.

Frank's reading also shows the depth of this new education. George Whitfield had an importance influence on John Wesley demonstrating to him the possibilities opened by preaching in the open air to the unchurched.

John Cennick was an early fruit of Methodism's ability to use lay people to spread the gospel. He had been converted in 1737 and begun a religious society in Reading. He was recruited by Wesley for full time teaching at the newly found Methodist school at Kingswood and joined him in preaching to local colliers [lxviii].

[lxiv] *Bebbington p11.* [lxv] *J&L Vol I 721,123-124 and notes.* [lxvi] *Bebbington p22.* [lxvii] *Bebbington p21.* [lxviii] *Baker p82.*

Frank goes on to describe how he started attending Methodist meetings in Wednesbury with the encouragement of his mother. He quickly devoured the opportunities which Methodism offered.

At Wednesbury Frank heard John Fletcher, one of Wesleys closest associates, who became the Vicar of Madeley in Shropshire, and had a profound influence on Methodism with his writings, especially over the controversial issue of predestination which he opposed.

Another speaker at Wednesbury was Benjamin Ingham, one of Methodism's first itinerant evangelists. He was with John Wesley in the Holy Club at Oxford and had accompanied him to Georgia in 1735. He became a pioneer evangelist in the north and in 1741 had married Lady Margaret Hastings, sister of the Earl of Huntingdon, whose widow the Countess of Huntingdon, was to play a great part in the establishment of Methodism.

When Frank was fifteen, in 1760, Alexander Mather, a Scots baker and itinerant preacher, was based in Wednesbury. His prayer meetings drew large crowds and led to a revival of the local society which Frank would have seen at first hand.

It is believed that both Frank and Richard Whatcoat – another future Bishop of the American Methodist Church who was based in Wednesbury – heard John Wesley preach in March of that year. It is quite possible that Eliza and other Methodists from West Bromwich and Great Barr would have been present on such an important occasion.

John Cennick.

Benjamin Ingham.

Frank joined a Methodist class at Bromwich Heath which was very close to the West Bromwich church and met in "band" with a group of other young people of his age in Wednesbury.

There were five young men in this band – Frank, his neighbour Thomas Ault, James Mayo, James Bayley and Thomas Russell. Thomas Ault described a typical Sunday "I became acquainted with Frank Asbury. He and me and three or four more used to go to Wednesbury in morning of the Lord's Day to the preaching at 8 of the clock, and when that was over, twice to West Bromwich church and at 5 in the evening to Wednesbury again" [lxix] Some sources say that at first the Methodist societies used to begin their meetings as early as 5 am!

Eliza Asbury gave her son every encouragement at every possible opportunity. Eliza set the example of reading. Eliza encouraged him to seek help from Ryland and it was Eliza that encouraged Frank to seek out the Wednesbury Methodists.

[lxix] *Autobiographical letter to Joseph Reeves 14 May 1821, quoted FW Hackwood, " West Bromwich", 1895, p227.*

6. "The People Called Methodists"

Eliza's conversion came at an exciting time for Christianity in England. John Wesley and others were criss-crossing the country preaching the message of salvation and establishing local Methodist societies.

Wesley never intended these societies to rival the local established Church of England and meetings were timed to enable Methodists to attend the parish church for communion.

Nevertheless Methodism experienced tremendous growth. From a handful of followers in the 1740s it had grown to 22,410 when records were first kept in 1767 to 88,334 in 1800 and on to a quarter of a million by 1830 [lxx].

We know that during her breakdown little help was forthcoming from the local church, St Margaret's at Great Barr. The congregation would have been dominated by local farmers who had their own designated pew as part of their lease agreement with the Gough family. Frank Asbury himself described the clergyman there as "our blind priest".

Most newly formed Methodist Societies met at first in private houses, but soon grew to such a size that they had to find premises [lxxi]. "We find that several converts in West Bromwich and elsewhere, threw open their houses for the meetings of the society as soon as formed there. At these meetings the brethren came together for prayer, singing hymns, and reading the scriptures" [lxxii].

Among those who "threw open their houses" were the Asburys. The small hamlet of Newton would never provide a large congregation but the cottage preaching house appeared on the Birmingham circuit plan for at least fifty years [lxxiii]. Occasionally, however Eliza Asbury and her friend Mrs Foxall would join the society at West Bromwich. Doubtless Eliza was there when her son preached his last sermon in the area before leaving for America in 1771 [lxxiv].

All Saints Church, sometimes referred to as "Old Church" at Bromwich Heath to the west across the Tame valley, was actually nearer to the Newton hamlet than the Great Barr parish Church, St Margaret's.

Of the period before the Methodist revival All Saints own historian recalls "…religion at this time was at a very low ebb; the clergy were men of bad character who neglected their work; church attendance was very poor indeed; and the people were given up to the not very edifying occupations of bull-baiting, dog fighting and cock fighting.

[lxx] Bebbington p21 quoting Currie "Churches and Churchgoers" Oxford 1977 p139. [lxxi] Davies "Methodism" Epworth 1963. [lxxii] Hackwood "West Bromwich" 1895 p222. [lxxiii] PWHS Vol 11 p102. [lxxiv] Hackwood "West Bromwich" 1895 p229.

"In 1742 Charles Wesley preached for the first time at Holloway Bank, which was then in West Bromwich parish, though very near to the Wednesbury border. At his request his brother John came in January of the following year, and as a result of this visit the first society of Methodists in the district was formed.

"It must be remembered that the Wesley's were both priests in the Church of England and that Methodist Societies at this time were guilds within the Church.

"The Vicar of Wednesbury was at first very friendly to the Methodist preachers, though he seems to have become hostile later; but the Vicar of West Bromwich was less favourably disposed.

"When John Wesley was preaching in April 1743 a clergyman who was 'very drunk' rode up on horseback and after many unseemly words tried to trample hearers under foot; there can be very little doubt that the clergyman was John Rann, who was then the unworthy Vicar of Old Church" [lxxv].

Twenty years later and the picture at All Saints had completely changed. The main local landowners were the Legge family, ennobled to the Earldom of Dartmouth for their support of the Stuarts during the Civil War and subsequent restoration [lxxvi]. William who was born in 1731, succeeded his grandfather in 1750. He was rare among the landed gentry in being a Methodist and a member of the Wednesbury Society, where he insisted on being known as "Brother Dartmouth".

Dartmouth used his patronage to secure the Vicarage at All Saints for Edward Stillingfleet, an ordained priest sympathetic to the Methodist movement and the grandson of Bishop Edward Stillingfleet of Worcester. Edward Stillingfleet served at All Saints between 1757 and 1782.

Both the Reverend Stillingfleet through the church, and Dartmouth through his political connections, were to play key roles in the gathering problems between Methodism and the established Church [lxxvii]. Dartmouth has a further claim on our attention by resigning as Secretary of State for the Colonies when war with the American colonists became inevitable.

At All Saints, Dartmouth and Vicar Stillingfleet were able to provide a structure close to Wesley's ideal. The Methodist society remained very much part of the parish, providing a platform and support for the growing corps of Methodist preachers. Meanwhile the parish church welcomed visiting ordained clergy of the established church, each sympathetic to the Methodist and evangelical cause.

West Bromwich, itself, then known as Bromwich Heath, was still centred on the area immediately around the church. Much of what we now call West Bromwich, towards the modern town centre, was still open heathland.

The Methodist Society at West Bromwich met at "The Room" This was about twenty feet square with a pillar in the centre. Men sat to the right of the preacher,

<hr />

[lxxv] *Hartill p21.* [lxxvi] *Cutting from undated edition about 1865 of "The Birmingham Post".* [lxxvii] *See F Baker.*

7. *Music and Method*

Immediately after Eliza and Frank received their assurance we can understand why many converts felt able to maintain a commitment to the new Methodist movement, Frank especially was caught in a whirlwind of activity.

First there were the house and cottage meetings: "I then held meetings frequently in my father's house, exhorting the people there, as also at Sutton Coldfield, and several souls professed to find peace through my labours. I met class awhile at Bromwich Heath and met in band at Wednesbury". All this in addition to his work as an apprentice!

The many activities of the new Methodist societies were carefully regulated. New converts such as Frank were quickly assigned to membership of a "class".

The class system came about almost by accident. In 1742 Methodists in Bristol needed to collect money regularly to pay for their new meeting room. One member suggested that the society membership be divided into lists of eleven with a leader appointed to collect a penny a week. It was when the leaders began to report back to Wesley the difficulties faced by those on the list, that Wesley realised the potential of the "class".

John Wesley called together the leaders and asked for regular reports on the progress being made by individuals within the class. He then tried the system out in London "Evil men were detected and reproved. They were borne with for a season. If they forsook their sins we received them gladly; if they obstinately persisted therein, it was openly declared that they were not one of us. The rest mourned and prayed for them, and rejoiced, that as far as they lay, the scandal was rolled away from the Society."

Leaders were instructed to see each person in his class at least once a week to advise, reprove, comfort, exhort and receive subscriptions for the poor. Then they were to meet the ministers and stewards to report progress and pay over the subscriptions.

John Wesley.

At first the leaders visited members in their own home, but this proved to be impractical. Classes then began to meet on a weekly basis. At each meeting a "full enquiry was made into the behaviour of every person". Advice and reproof was given when required, quarrels made up, misunderstandings removed. Members bought together learnt to bear one another's burdens and gradually developed a bond of friendship, meetings lasted between one or two hours and concluded with prayer and a hymn lxxxiii.

The classes consisted of between nine and eighteen members, chosen on a geographical basis, which explains why Frank was in a class at West Bromwich, which was nearer to the cottage at Newton than was Wednesbury lxxxiv.

The classes were divided by sex and this led to women playing an important leadership role in the societies from the very start. As we will see later the involvement of women in the movement's leadership women caused problems for the societies in Wednesbury and West Bromwich.

The leaders were often people of humble background and little education. The classes provided important training for future lay leaders both within the church and the wider community. What happened in each meeting inevitably varied from place to place. Much of the discussion was of a very personal, even intimate nature. There were opportunities for prayer, testimony and confession. Those who were old or sick were visited and where necessary given financial support lxxxv.

The "ticket", renewed every quarter, ensured that the societies could discard disorderly members. Each member was interviewed and enquiries made of leaders and neighbours whether they "grew in grace". The ticket was, according to Wesley, the equivalent of stating "I believe the bearer hereof to be one that fears God and works righteousness." No new ticket meant they were no longer part of the Methodist community lxxxvi.

Frank was also a member of a "band", which, met at Wednesbury. Wesley had instructed that male bands met on Wednesday evenings and women bands met on Sunday lxxxvii. Bands were divided by sex and marital status lxxxviii.

Frank Asbury met "in band" with four other young men of about the same age, 15 or 16 years old. Bands had a greater intensity than either the classes or the society meetings. Methodists felt themselves under attack : "They had still to wrestle both with flesh and blood, and with principalities and powers, so that temptation were on every side and often temptation of such a kind, as they knew not how to speak in a class.." explained Wesley lxxxix.

A band, which was probably self selecting, undertook to meet weekly, confess to one another, pray for mutual healing, sing and pray.

---

lxxxiii *Wesley p6-8.* lxxxiv *Bebbington, "By 1783 in Bristol there were fifty seven classes, each including from nine to eighteen members. The allocation of classes was on a purely geographical basis" p24.* lxxxv *Davies p63.* lxxxvi *Wesley p10.* lxxxvii *Wesley p12.* lxxxviii *Bebbington Ibid p24.* lxxxix *Wesley p11.*

The four young men who met with Frank went on to become leading members of the local Methodist societies and kept contact with Frank and with Joseph and Eliza throughout their lives.

Thomas Ault, a shoemaker, served both the Methodist society and his parish church; for most of his life he lived next door to "The Room" in Paradise Street, West Bromwich, whilst his father moved from Newton to Spon Lane, the road connecting West Bromwich with Smethwick.

James Mayo; succeeded Frank as leader of the West Bromwich class when Frank became an itinerant preacher, until he moved to Birmingham.

James Bayley was a park-keeper on Dartmouth's Sandwell estate for forty seven years and died in December 1798 at the age of 71. Thomas Russell was a carpenter, lived in Overend and died shortly after Bayley [xc].

Apart from the bands and classes there would have been many other activities for these young men and their parents.

Should the society leadership believe a member was "backsliding", then they were invited to special "penitent" meetings on Saturday evenings with hymns and readings carefully chosen to encourage them and rekindle their faith.

Over three evenings each quarter the entire society would gather for a "love feast" where bread or buns would be passed around and water drank from a common cup. The men would meet on the first evening, the women on the second and the whole society on a third [xci].

Monthly watchnight services, usually on the Friday evening closest to the full moon for the light were voluntary, with numerous other preaching and teaching meetings.

Highlights of Methodist life were the visits by John Wesley himself. There is no record that he ever preached in Barr or visited the Asbury cottage, although in February 1744 as he travelled from Birmingham to Stafford he was caught in a ferocious storm as he passed through the area [xcii].

However he visited Wednesbury and West Bromwich on many occasions. No doubt Eliza would have wanted to hear him and helped to swell the congregations of the neighbouring society. He records his visits in his journals:

"Sunday March 20, 1768 - About one I preached on West Bromwich Heath; in the evening near the Preaching House in Wednesbury. The north wind cut like a razor, but the congregation as well as me had something else to think of.

"Sunday March 18, 1770 – At half hour after one I was to preach at Bromwich Heath, but the House would scarce contain a fourth part of the congregation, so I made a virtue of necessity, and preached in a ground where there was room for all that came, and I believe God kindled a fire in many frozen hearts.

[xc] *Hackwood "West Bromwich" 1895 p227.* [xci] *Wesley p12 & 13.* [xcii] *Woodall p22.*

"Sunday March 20, 1774 – At noon I preached on Bromwich Heath, and the Room being far too small, stood in Mr Wiley's courtyard (that is the Oak House in West Bromwich), notwithstanding the keen north-east wind.

"Sunday March 21, 1779 – Just at the time of preaching at Bromwich Heath, began such a storm as that which ushered in the year. Yet as no house could contain the people, I was constrained to stand in the courtyard. For a moment I was afraid of the tiles falling on the people, but they regarded nothing but the word; as I concluded, we had a furious shower of hail: Hitherto could the prince of the power of the air go, but no further."

One of Eliza's contemporaries, John Sanders, recalled following him to each of three preaching appointments on one day. In the morning Wesley spoke at Wednesbury, then in the afternoon in Dudley and in the evening Wolverhampton. As Sanders and his companions were walking from Dudley to Wolverhampton, Wesley overtook them, and recognising them as young Methodists asked his coachmen to drive slowly, put his head through the window and spoke to them [xciii].

Much of the emotion, enthusiasm and teaching of Methodism was expressed in the hymns of Charles Wesley, brother of John. The hymns were collected together in a series of hymnbooks published in 1737, 1741, 1753 and 1780 [xciv]. Each hymn was carefully written, to express Methodist doctrine. Some were taken from other sources which were consistent with Methodist theology, for example they included "Ye Holy Angels Bright", which had been written by Richard Baxter from Kidderminster.

Much of the verse summarised the very personal nature of a conviction of sin, conversion, assurance of faith and the hope of Christian perfection. It is possible to see why someone with Eliza Asbury's experience would find them a great help and encouragement. One was written soon after Charles Wesley had his own experience of assurance [xcv]:

Where shall my wondering soul begin
How shall I all to heaven aspire
A slave redeemed from death and sin
A brand plucked from eternal fire [xcvi]

The Wesley's went to great lengths to find the best tunes. Some were specially written by friends, others were well established psalm tunes. Some were adaptations of operatic tunes or favourite songs. One of the most famous Wesley hymns "Love Divine, All Loves Excelling" was written by Charles after hearing a Purcell tune which he believed deserved a better subject [xcvii].

xciii John Sanders original MS taken by Samuel Lees 1860. Sandwell MBC archives. xciv John Telford "The Methodist Hymn Book Illustrated" Epworth 1934 pvi. xcv Telford p192. xcvi Hymn 706 "Hymns and Psalms". xcvii Davies p97.

"Love Divine" is just one of the many Wesley hymns which have been absorbed by every Christian denomination of every nationality. The simplicity and evident sincerity of the words make it a favourite at wedding services, though the urgency of the Methodist theology comes through.

Although slightly altered from the form in which it was first published it is easy to see why it has an enduring appeal. The first verse highlights the love, joy, mercy and awe of Jesus's compassion

Love divine, all loves excelling'
Joy of heaven to earth come down,
Fix in us thy humble dwelling,
All thy faithful mercies crown.
Jesu though art all compassion,
Pure unbounded love thou art;
Visit us with thy salvation,
Enter every trembling heart.

The second verse earnestly calls on God for real assurance

Come, almighty to deliver
Let us all thy life receive;

And the third verse seeks Christian perfection and looks to the gift of eternal life:

Finish then thy new creation
Pure and spotless let us be;
Let us see thy great salvation
Perfectly restored in thee:
Changed from glory into glory,
Till in heaven we take our place,
Till we cast our crowns before thee,
Lost in wonder, love and praise [xcviii].

Other Wesley hymns still sung in the 21st Century include the Christmas Carol "Hark the Herald Angels Sing" and the Easter Hymn "Jesus Christ is Risen Today".

John Wesley made it clear that he saw singing as important part of the expression of Christianity. He issued clear "Directions to Singers" in the 1770 hymn book:

[xcviii] *Hymn 267 "Hymns and Psalms".*

"Sing *all*. Let not a slight degree of weakness or weariness hinder you. If it is a cross to you, take it up and you will find it a blessing.

"Sing *lustily* and with good courage. Beware of singing as if you are half dead or half asleep; but lift up your voice with strength. Be no more afraid of your voice now, nor more ashamed of being heard, than when you sing the songs of Satan.

"Sing *modestly*. Strive to unite your voices together so as to make one clear melodious sound.

"Sing in *tune*, and take care not to sing too slow. This drawling way naturally steals on all who are lazy; and it is high time to drive it from among us, and sing all our tunes just as quick as we did at first.

"Above all sing *spiritually*. Have an eye to God in every word you sing. Attend strictly to the sense of what you sing, and see that your heart is not carried away with the sound, but offered to God continually" [xcix].

Eliza's contemporary John Sanders recalled that "Mr John Wesley was always very particular about the singing and would have people sing in time and tune. I remember one day hearing him at Wednesbury. There was a large congregation and suddenly Mr Wesley put up his hand and they all stopped. He said you are bleating like cows in that corner and there is a man in that gallery who has been singing a false note. The faults were mended and the singing went on [c].

[xcix] *Quoted Davies p98.* [c] *John Sanders original MS taken by Samuel Lees 1860. Sandwell MBC archives.*

8. Under Attack

The new Methodist societies met several challenges. For many years there remained the external threat of anti-Methodist rioting. Serious incidents continuing well into the 1760s in both Birmingham, Wolverhampton and other towns. The West Bromwich society may have missed much of this persecution because it enjoyed the patronage and protection of Dartmouth and Stillingfleet.

There were sharp disagreements with other non-conformist groups which continued well after the riots of the 1740s. West Bromwich itself was, according to the local historian Reeves "at that time and for many years afterwards, over run with antinomians".

The antinomian theology is best described by their favourite slogan: they were "perfect in Christ, not in themselves". One John Ward, alias Mouse-trap Ward, contended that he could take any article out of a shop if he needed it and had a right to all the women of the world if only they would consent. As late as 1776 John Wesley was to complain that "I preached at Dudley in the midst of antinomians and backsliders".

The local Baptists with their theology of predestination also presented opposition. A frustrated John Wesley was to complain "What a work would have been done in these parts if it had not been for doubtful disputants! If the Predestinarians had not thrown back those who began to run well, partly to the world, partly to the Baptists, and partly into endless disputes concerning the secret counsels of God.

"While we carried our lives in our hands, none of them came near; the waves ran too high for them. But when all was calm, they poured in on all sides and bereaved us of our children. Out of these they formed one society here, one at Dudley and another at Birmingham. Many indeed, though torn from us, would not stay with them, but broke into wildest enthusiasm. But still they were called Methodists; so all their drunkenness and blasphemies were imputed to us" [ci].

Many of the problems were internal to the Methodist movement. It should be remembered that many of the early Methodists were ill educated [cii], worked in appalling conditions, had limited experiences of Church or organisation, and often became Methodists after a dramatic personal battle as had Eliza Asbury.

As early as 1751 John Wesley had to expel antinomian James Wheatley from the West Bromwich Society. Wheatley tried to establish an independent society in Norwich, returned to West Bromwich and spent the five years between 1759 and 1764 trying to set up a rival preaching house in Paradise Street for which he was said to have collected

[ci] *Hackwood "West Bromwich" 1895 p221.* [cii] *Davies p78.*

£20 [ciii]. Two members of Frank Asbury's Band, James Bayley and Joseph Russell subsequently bought the property, finished the building and opened it as a Methodist preaching room.

One of Wesley's Preachers in Norwich, Thomas Mitchell, complained "I had many trials from J. Wheatley's people. Mr Wesley had been prevailed upon to take the tabernacle and to receive Wheatley's people under his care. Wheatley called them "my dear lambs"; but such lion like lambs did I never see.

"Discipline they knew nothing of, everyone would do what was right in his own eyes. And our own doctrine was an abomination to them. Great part of them were grounded in antinomianism. The very sound of perfection they abhorred; they hardly knew the word "holiness". Nothing was pleasing to them but "faith, faith"; without a word either of its inward or outward fruits [civ].

Another preacher, Alexander Mather, who played an important part in the call of Frank Asbury to preach and teach recalled the internal problems which beset the often struggling communities of Methodists.

At first in the early 1760s the threat was from outside.

"...the societies increased greatly. In Darlaston we purchased ground and built a preaching house; and in Birmingham we hired a large building. Satan was alarmed at this, and stirred up outward persecution both at Birmingham and Wolverhampton. But it did us no hurt. Our brethren went on, not counting their lives dear unto themselves."

But then the set of problems were much more insidious:

"He (Satan) then made the minds of some of the old Methodists evil affected towards their brethren. They began to speak much evil, particularly in their classes of them and of this new doctrine. And any defects in these new converts (as they called them) was magnified to the utmost and then brought as undeniable proof that the whole thing was wrong.

"These were earnestly supported by Mr J–s, formerly an itinerant, now a local preacher. To him they sent every tale that malice could invent, either against the work, of the instruments employed therein, my wife in particular: whom indeed, God had been pleased to make eminently useful.

Alexander Mather.

[ciii] *Hackwood " West Bromwich" 1895 p229.* [civ] *"Lives of Early Methodist Preachers" Vol 1 p56.*

"This embarrassed me a little: however we went on, and the work did not suffer much until about the time of the Conference, when some of the preachers going through the Circuit, and hearing only one side, (though they might have heard both as I was present) both privately encouraged the opposition and in their public discourses, dividing the people into the new and old believers, used many unkind expressions, to encourage the old and discourage the new believers as they called them."

Mather accepted that he made a false step which he regretted and which highlighted a distinctive feature of eighteenth century Methodism of which Eliza Asbury came to exemplify:

" ...longing for peace, and preferring the judgement of other men to my own. I agreed that my wife should not hold anymore prayer meetings. Immediately the work began to decay both as its extensiveness and usefulness. And though I continued to insist as strongly as ever on the same points, yet there was not the same effect for want of seconding by prayer meetings the blow which was given in preaching" cv.

The story of Mather's wife being banned from holding prayer meetings is ironic, given that Susannah Wesley, mother of John and Charles, met similar opposition when her husband was Rector at Epworth in Lincolnshire. Susannah held meetings in her kitchen which were more popular than the formal services provided by the curate at her husband's church.

Women were numerous in the early Methodist movement. Some research shows that more than half the members of some societies were women, with nearly half of them unmarried.

As both Mrs Mather and Elizabeth Asbury demonstrated, they were not necessarily kept in the background. Outside of formal church settings "women found opportunities for self expression. In the proliferating cottage meetings of early Evangelicalism it was often the women who took the lead in prayer and praise, counsel and exhortation" cvi.

A growing problem within the Methodist societies was the relationship with the established Church of England. This was to be particularly felt within the Methodist Society at West Bromwich, amongst some of Eliza Asbury's closest friends.

There was always a pressure from some Methodists, particularly those that had come from a dissenting background, to establish an entirely separate church. Much of this was contained so long as John Wesley lived.

In West Bromwich the incumbency of Stillingfleet played a major part in providing local Methodists with good reason to stay within the establish church. One West Bromwich Methodist, a childhood friend of Frank, Thomas Ault, served as parish clerk. He left Methodism when the local society stopped attending All Saints, following Stillingfleet's retirement.

cv *Lives Vol I p271.* cvi *Bebbington p26.*

The irony of Asbury's ordination was not lost on the congregation of All Saints. The Church's historian dryly remarks "..thus the West Bromwich Methodist Class provided one of the most prominent leaders of the Methodism which broke away from the English Church [cvii].

Thomas Ault met again with the Methodists in later life until his death in 1825. His nephew William entered the Methodist ministry in 1808 and sailed with Thomas Coke for Ceylon in 1814. Coke died during the voyage and William just a year after landing [cviii].

Despite this opposition, Methodism in West Bromwich grew along with its population. By the 1830s there were 18 Wesleyan Chapels and schools providing accommodation for 3550 worshippers, 10 Sunday schools for 1375

Thomas Coke.

children and a day school for 280. By 1849 the Primitive Methodist connexion (that is the name given for an organisation of Methodist churches) had set up a West Bromwich circuit which added another fifteen chapels providing accommodation for 4,000, supported by 30 local preachers [cix].

One hundred years after Elizabeth Asbury's conversion West Bromwich had a population of about 28,000 [cx] and enough room in its Methodist chapels and school rooms to accommodate over 9,205 at any one time – nearly a third of the population.

[cvii] *Harthill p21.* [cviii] *MWHS Vol I p13-14 1965.* [cix] *Hackwood "West Bromwich" 1895 p233-224 quoting James Hall, "Methodism in West Bromwich 1742-1885".* [cx] *Based Ede Ibid Appendix 1 West Bromwich's population in 1841 was 26,100, by 1851 it had grown to 34,600.*

9. The Growing Son

Frank wrote having felt "something of God as early as the age of seven"[cxi]. Joseph was evidently disappointed that he didn't stay at school beyond the age of thirteen. Frank Asbury's conversion to a whole hearted Christian faith between the age of fourteen and sixteen, had far reaching consequences for Joseph and Eliza.

Within months Frank had already left work as an apprentice in service to "one of the wealthiest and most ungodly families we had in the parish". In that position said Frank "I became vain, but not openly wicked". Who that employer was, is discreetly lost in the mist of time.

Frank then made the choice, at the age of thirteen and a half, to be apprenticed to a family where he was treated "more like a son or an equal than an employee" [cxii].

Who that employer was, is of some controversy. One of Frank Asbury's earliest biographers, Dr W.P. Strickland did not identify the employer, nor did Frank.

The earliest local historian Joseph Reeves identified the employer as John Griffin, a maker of chapes, small pieces of metal which were fixed around the top of top of a scabbard for a sword. Frank certainly enquired about a "Widow Griffin" in a letter to his cousin following his mother's death.

Henry Foxall.

However Frederick Briggs ministered in the Handsworth and Great Barr area in the mid 1800s and sought out the many local legends which had attached themselves to the Asbury family.

Briggs concluded that the employer was a man named Thomas Foxall who had recently migrated from Monmouthshire and had set up business at the Old Forge where to that day, in 1879, "the anvil on which Francis Asbury wrought is still reverently preserved as a precious memento of his providential early training".

Certainly the Old Forge Mill farm, now in the ownership of Sandwell Metropolitan Council and open to the public, was one of the closest of the water driven mills on the River Tame to the Newton home. Between 1742 and 1762 the Mill

[cxi] J&L Vol I p44. [cxii] J&L Vol I p721.

was leased from the Earl of Dartmouth by John Churchill. There is no documentary evidence to link Frank Asbury to this particular mill but it is a strong local legend, frequently repeated cxiii. For example a Mr Harry Newby is quoted by James Lewis in 1927 as saying that a Mr Foxall was the foreman blacksmith at the Old Forge, not far from where the Jubilee pit had been sunk cxiv.

This forge was more than a simple country blacksmith's shop. The River Tame divided the plateau upon which Birmingham was situated and that upon which sat Wednesbury. Although a gentle, non-navigable river, the Tame, and its contributories, provided the motive power for many small forges fired by local coal.

The products of each mill varied with the demand. Sometimes the mill would

Old Forge Mill Farm, Sandwell Valley. Reputed home of the Foxall family to whom Frank was believed to be apprenticed and who regularly worshipped at the Asbury Cottage.

concentrate on their original function of milling corn, on other occasions they would be turned over to providing the power for the ever growing metal industry in the days before steam power became common. Whilst the ownership of the mills remained firmly in the hands of the local landowners, the mill operations were rented out to contractors.

The Old Forge Mill was a slitting mill. It was a comparatively small operation employing four people, one of whom was the foreman, presumably for a time, Thomas Foxall. The mill could process just three tons of iron a day owing to the lack of adequate water power cxv.

A good preserved example of such a mill, though on the Cole not the Tame, is Sarehole Mill in south Birmingham, which is open to the public as museum. In the twentieth century Sarehole Mill found fresh fame as the home of Bilbo and Frodo Baggins in the book and film "The Lord of the Rings" written by local author J.R.R. Tolkien.

One metal trade which would have been practised at the Old Forge was nail making. This trade was especially easy to enter and attracted migrant workers, one of whom could have been Foxall.

Certainly the Foxall family became firm friends of the Asburys. Mrs Foxall became very close to Eliza and joined her at the weekly cottage meetings. Frank's first sermon at Manwoods was just a quarter of a mile from the Old Forge.

cxiii *Dilworth p47.* cxiv *Lewis p17.* cxv *Dilworth p48.*

The Foxall's son Henry, was born about the time that Frank started working for them in 1758. Henry Foxall went to America and is mentioned several times in Frank's journal and letters.

He took his metal skills with him and set up an armoury, making guns for the new United States army. His designs were so advanced that half a century later the first salvos of the American Civil War were from Foxall cannons in Fort Sumter. The Old Forge may well be the cradle of the US arms industry.

Manwoods cottage, where Frank first preached, demolished some time between 1874 and 1900.

In her one surviving letter Elizabeth Asbury enquires of Henry Foxall's health. She also gives news of Edward Jordan and his wife who were passing on their best wishes to Henry through Frank, additionally mentioning the progress of Henry's brothers John and Benjamin [cxvi].

Henry was an enthusiastic Methodist who helped fund a church in Georgetown, and provided Frank with financial assistance and occasional lodgings. Whilst visiting England in 1823 he fell ill and was buried in the grounds of the All Saints, Bromwich Heath. The entry in the parish register notes that he was Mayor of Georgetown, Washington DC 1819-1823 and a "Friend of Asbury" [cxvii].

In the eighteenth century formal apprenticeships were taxed and the records of this taxation are now with the Society of Geneologists in London. There is no Asbury listed so that line of enquiry is closed.

The truth about Frank's apprenticeship may well be that he worked for both John Griffin and Thomas Foxall. This could have been at the same time, or in sequence.

Earlier researchers such as Briggs may have made the same initial mistake as the Birmingham historian Hutton and misunderstood the nature of the "blacksmith's" work in the area. At the Old Forge, Foxall would have been producing the small manageable pieces of metal that would have been used in Birmingham's "toy trade", such as that used by button makers, or chape makers or the gun trade. John Griffiths and Thomas Foxall would have used the same raw materials and were based just a few hundred yards from one another along the River Tame.

[cxvi] *J&L Vol III, p184, Donovan.* [cxvii] *"Register of Burials in the parish of West Bromwich in the County of Staffordshire in the Year 1823" entry number 1803 dated December 16.*

10. The Itinerant Son

In 1766, when Frank was twenty one, he was ready to leave home and join John Wesley's team of itinerant Methodist preachers. This was not an easy year in the Midlands, with the urban areas being convulsed by a series of 'hunger strikes'. Initially Frank filled in for another preacher in the area between Staffordshire and Gloucester who had fallen ill [cxviii]. During that period of his work he could have regularly passed and stayed at the Newton home.

This period was evidently not without difficulty for the new itinerant. The Rev William Orpe wrote to him from Darlaston rebuking him for not paying enough attention to his work. There had apparently been a problem with missed meetings.

Frank was in Hampton (this could be in Shropshire or Warwickshire) at the time. "You have lost enough by gazing all around; for God's sake do so no more". Orpe then asked to see Frank the following Sunday in Wednesbury where he ominously says "I have a little concern to mention. I hope you'll call." Quite what the little concern was it is not possible to discover, but this letter indicates that Frank was taking some time in settling into the new role [cxix].

But Frank impressed those who heard him. One Thomas Slater in Derbyshire remembered Frank as "Then a youth not quite out of his teens with a voice like a roaring lion" [cxx].

Wesley kept his young preachers on the move. The following year Frank travelled in Bedfordshire and Sussex and then in 1768 to Colchester with a time in Wiltshire. In 1769 he was re-appointed to Bedfordshire and Northamptonshire, and then to his final posting in England, based in Salisbury, Wiltshire in 1770 [cxxi].

During his years in England Frank kept in touch with his mother and the society based at

Painting by Eric Jennings, depicting Frank Asbury leaving Salisbury in 1771.

[cxviii] Briggs p22. [cxix] J&L Vol III p10. [cxx] PWHS Vol 16. [cxxi] Briggs op cit p23; J&L Vol I p125.

"Friend Thomas Smith" was asked "where are you?" and urged " Yet out of Christ, host of Christ, shake yourself from the dust, arise and fly to Jesus, the city of refuge. Make haste my dear friend, make haste, the avenger of blood is at your heels".

Molly Sheldon was told, with some words effaced from the original, "there is nothing but complaining in your streets and maybe you are ready to say ——— I doubt there never will be a child, you are like the woman with a bloody issue that spent all she had and now no better......Oh may you be driven by extreme want to him and fall nigh.

"To my friend Sheldon, Oh my dear heart where are you? Tossed like a ship upon the ocean, here and there, but no rest. Return to Jesus weeping to Him and give a divorce to your sins..." This may be a reference to John Sheldon who suffered in the Wednesbury riots and had moved on to become a tenant of Balls Hill Farm and was now of some substance [cxxiv].

"To Mother Perkins, do you love Jesus? Do you increase with the increase of God? If so watch and pray and go home and prosper.

"To Betty Wilkes, are you following the humble Nazarene, Jesus the joy and desire of the whole Christ above and below? Oh go on, pray and watch, and hate the thing that is evil, and God, even you have God, shall give you his blessing and care for your soul and body.

"To Sarah Weston, I hope it will be given you to go through evil report and good and be a faithful follower of the Lamb which your soul wishes and desires and prays for you, my dear heart...My love to John. I wish and desire and pray that he may have repentance and remission of sins, that both your souls may be bound up in the bundle of life..."

But the most interesting references are to those with the surname Brooks. He urges Mrs Brookes to "See the victory...Do you find comfort in Jesus and stay your soul upon Him? You may answer to this but I am weak and the world follows and sticks close. Look to the strong for strength, He the Lord will free you from this plague of earth this moment. Oh cry to you God this moment".

The note to Sally Brooks contains concern that her "hard heart is broken and that the hand of God presses your love, that you give up every vanity..." But then Frank adds "That you must not expect me to write very often, it is so far, send me a letter quick."

It may be that Sally Brooks wrote on behalf of Eliza and Joseph or that there was some special friendship between Frank and Sally – no one else addressed in the letter is invited to write to him.

There however appears to have been some romantic link between Frank and another local woman, also called Brookes, known as Nancy. Frank addresses her too within the letter to his parents.

[cxxiv] *Letter in Samuel Lees collection. Sandwell MBC archives.*

"Nancy Brookes, your manner of speaking made me begin to think and wonder. I know very well that it becomes me to be without partiality and if you or any other will convince me of it I would be ashamed of it, and shake it off as I would the mire of the streets.

"I don't say but I may be guilty of it, but I do not know wherein and in regard to what passed when I was over at Barr, I can't tell wherein and it is a pity, but you had told me or would do it.

"My time was short. I was with all the people but you, I think, and also I was at your house but you were not at home.

"I could [have] been glad of your company as any at Barr, and wanted it but could not have it, but my dear heart I shall think no more of it if you don't, tho it gave me some little pain. For who is offended, and I burn not. Dear Child I travailed in birth for you and never sought any ——— [letter torn] God is my witness, but his glory and your good.

"And tho you have ten thousand instructors in Christ, you have not many fathers for in Christ I have begotten you a lively hope. My dear child, I am jealous over you with a godly jealousy, lest as the serpent beguiled Eve, you should be drawn from the simplicity of the gospel."

Local legend says that Eliza Asbury did not see Nancy as a suitable match for Frank. Many years later Frank conceded that being single was an advantage and included "what once befell me in England", often taken as a reference to the relationship with Nancy [cxxv].

Eliza and Joseph Asbury took the opportunity to visit their son when he was stationed in Bedfordshire and possibly Hampshire. In a later letter dated 20 July 1770, notable for its references to some of the difficulties he was then facing him, Frank refers to those who asked to be remembered to them.

"Most who know you ask after you, and give their love to you – Miss Tyers in particular, and her mother, and Mrs Spencer. I read those lines to Betty Gent and her husband, and both of them seemed much affected.

"I have been most of my time in Bedfordshire since you left me. Mr England's people are well. They have had the things you sent them; not one is broken" [cxxvi].

Apparently during a visit to Hampshire Eliza Asbury left a strong impression on four women in Whitchurch Hampshire. When they heard that Frank had agreed to go to America at the Bristol conference in August 1771 they immediately wrote to Eliza Asbury – not to Joseph or to them both – asking that she dissuade Frank from going.

[cxxv] *J&L Vol III p6 & 36.* [cxxvi] *J&L Vol III p8.*

The letter read

"Whitchurch, August 27, 1771

"Dear Mrs Asbury,

"We have heard that your son is going, or has gone to America. We expected he would call on us, to bid us farewell. But as the time is expired, we must give up our hope.

"So we have troubled you with a few lines, by way of inquiry if you were willing to part with him, and he willing to part from you? We think it must be an instance of much trouble to both, for indeed we were very much grieved when we heard Mr Asbury was going there.

"The intent of writing this is to beg the favour of you to send us a few lines, as soon as possible, that we may be informed of the particulars of this long journey, if he is gone; for we scarce believe he is so mad, and to desire another letter from you the first time he writes to you from abroad.

"Indeed the Lord has made him a useful instrument to many here, and he will not be easily forgotten by us. Indeed, our sister, you have great reason to rejoice in the Lord, in that your son is also a son of God, and an heir with the Lord in glory.

"But this is no doubt a time of distress to you and your husband; and we in some measure mourn with you for the loss of him for so long a time.

"But we hope the Lord will restore him again in peace, to the joy of your hearts. We all join in respectful love to you, and remain

"Your affectionate sisters,

"S. Faithorn, Mary Farmer, M. Butler, Elizabeth Web

"P.S. Pray send as soon as possible. Direct to Mrs Faithorn, Whitchurch, Hants" cxxvii.

In late August 1771 Frank made his way back to the cottage to say his farewells to both parents and friends. Being their only surviving child it must have been a difficult few days for them.

Frank believed he raised the subject of his stationing in America to them "in as gentle a manner as possible. Though it was grievous to flesh and blood, they consented to let me go. My mother is one of the tenderest people in the world; but I believe, she was blessed in the present instance with Divine assistance to part with me.

cxxvii *J&L Vol III p9-10.*

"I visited most of my friends in Staffordshire, Warwickshire and Gloucestershire, and felt much life and power among them. Several of our meetings were indeed held in the spirit and life of God.

"Many of my friends were struck with wonder, when they heard of my going; but none opened their mouths against it, hoping it was of God. Some wished that their situation would allow them to go with me" [cxxviii].

He preached a farewell sermon at a crowded meeting in the cottage [cxxix].

Frank's last evening in the Midlands was spent in "prayerful conversation" with Edward Hand a cordwainer and Methodist leader in Sutton Coldfield who was to suffer many years of persecution and harassment for his beliefs [cxxx].

The final farewell was especially difficult. His father was overwhelmed with grief and tears. Eliza, by contrast, was calm and self restrained.

Frank wished to leave his parents a keep sake. He had little, Methodist preachers were poorly paid and travelled lightly. He put his hand in his pocket and produced his silver watch which he gave to his parents as something to remember him by. Briggs reports that " Sobbing out his last farewell, he thrust his watch impulsively into his mother's hand and fled" [cxxxi].

After his father's death, Frank wrote of his leaving, "wounded memory recalls what took place when I parted with him, nearly twenty seven years ago next September; from a man that seldom, if ever, I saw weep – but when I came to America, overwhelmed with tears, with grief, he cried out, 'I shall never see him again'… " [cxxxii].

In 1771 Frank had just turned 26. Eliza and Joseph were 56 or 57.

Their son sailed from Pill near Bristol on Wednesday 4 September, a stone monument now marks the spot.

Neither Eliza nor Joseph were ever to see Frank again.

[cxxviii] *J&L Vol I p3-4.* [cxxix] *Reeves, J MWHS Vol I p11 (1965)* [cxxx] *Sheldon p5 and 9.* [cxxxi] *Briggs p23-24* [cxxxii] *J&L Vol II p162.*

11. Eliza's Second Bereavement

From the moment that Frank left for America, Eliza and Joseph mainly heard of his progress through his letters or through visitors, normally preachers, who had met him during his travels in America.

John Allen.

It is clear that Eliza took her son's departure badly. Frank recorded in October 1772, …This day I received a letter from my mother, informing me that she was weak in body, and had an earnest desire to see me once more before she dies" cxxxiii.

A surviving letter from John Allen, dated 26 January 1772, another itinerant preacher who had been based in Wednesbury, but had moved to London, shows that Eliza discussed her grief at the apparent loss of her son with others.

It is clear that all had the expectation that it was unlikely Eliza would see her son again.

John Allen begins by explaining that he was prompted to write by someone who had recently seen Eliza, once again it is addressed to her alone and not to her and Joseph:

"Dear Sister,

"Mrs Tilt informed me last night that she had seen you, and that you had desired that I would write you a letter which I am not unwilling to do, only I know not what to say that may be of any use to you. But as she is sending a parcel (in which case I can send this post free) I venture to send you a few lines.

"I have often thought of you since the Conference, on account of Frankey's going to America, which must have been a heavy trial for you, as you have no other child. However I rejoice to hear that you have been enabled to bear it pretty well, and doubt not but that this shall work together for your good.

"I doubt not that Frankey believed that it was the Will of God he should go, and therefore had the resolution 'to forsake father and mother' and his own native country to comply with the Will of God and am persuaded that God will 'not forget this his work of faith and Labour of Love'.

cxxxiii J&L Vol I p45.

" Tis true, that you may see him no more in this world, but through Perseverance, you shall see him to the Day of Eternity. Then be resigned to the will of heavens and sing 'Since this thy sinteneer should part, With what was nearest to my heart, I freely that and more resign, Behold my heart itself is thine! My little all I give to thee, Thou has bestowed thy son on me'

"While this is not the language of your heart you cannot be unhappy; nor, indeed, can you be really happy any longer than this is the case.

"If it lay in my power to make your life comfortable, I should rejoice to do it.

"I have a Regard for you, and love your son as I love my Brother. You are now in the decline of life, and your greatest wisdom will be to prepare every moment for your dissolution. Live to God more abundantly, and he will not forsake you when you are old and grey headed. Take Jesus for your present Father and your eternal Reward. Give him all your heart and all your life.

"Be of good courage and he will strengthen you in Soul. Fear not, only believe.

"God is good and delights to do you good, and will cause goodness and mercy to follow you all your days. He never leaves nor forsakes those that put their trust in him. He has been your God from your youth up, and he will be your guide unto death.

"I hope your Husband is earnestly seeking the salvation of his soul and endeavours to make your life comfortable. Give my love to him and all friends at Barr, pray that God may Bless you with more grace here and Glory hereafter, is the prayer of him, who is your affectionate brother in the Lord, John Allen."

Within years the American Revolution would be underway, communications broke down entirely and Eliza would be left to bear her grief with virtually no news of her son.

12. Letters from America before the War

Franks letters home before the War of Independence seemed to be aimed at a wider audience that just his parents. His descriptions of life in America may have been designed to encourage other Methodists, especially preachers, to join him.

Frank's lifestyle, often away from the city's and regular trade routes meant that it was very difficult for him to post and receive letters from his parents. The post travelled by sea and stage coach taking weeks, possibly months to arrive from either direction.

During the War of Independence contact stopped altogether for a period of about seven years [cxxxiv].

The West Midlands, particularly Birmingham, had good trade links with the American colonies which were quickly re-established after the cessation of the hostilities of the War of Independence. Frank addressed most of his letters to his father at his place of work, Hamstead Hall.

Frank's foremost concern for his parents, was their spiritual state. He often mentioned other issues – particularly money which he remitted to them at frequent intervals through the Methodist publishing concerns.

The first surviving letter was from New York and dated 7 October 1772, less than a year after arriving in America. It was in response to one from Eliza saying that she was poorly and wanted to see him before she died.

It appears that during those first few months the correspondence between parents and son was considerably more frequent than it was in later years.

During the same week Frank had pressing problems with his work. Frank disapproved of the local steward letting non-members into society meetings and had written to John Wesley about the situation the previous day. He refers "this was a day of peace and rest to my soul. After preaching at night with some power, I spoke to our steward, whose conduct did not altogether please me – frequently avoiding to speak to me – absenting himself from the meeting of the leaders – the appearance of dissimulation – opposing our rules – and consulting persons who were not members of our society. He appeared to be somewhat affected by the conversation" [cxxxv].

Frank's opening paragraph mentions that he had received two letters from them when he was in Philadelphia, but a third had been lost in New York. He says that he had sent four letters to them and enquires whether they had had a recent one sent from Philadelphia by way of Bristol.

[cxxxiv] *J&L Vol III p35.* [cxxxv] *J&L Vol I p45.*

His parents had evidently reassured him of their financial situation. "I am glad to hear you do not want for the things of life; for if you had wanted these it would trouble me much".

But he responded firmly to their request for him to return home:

"I cannot comply at present with your request, as I think it is not the order of God. You would not have me leave the work God hath called me to, for the dearest friend in life. If the flesh will, your spirit will not. However, you can depend upon it, I will come home as soon as I can: but he that believeth shall not make haste.

"As I did not come here without counsels and prayers, I hope not to return without them, lest I should be like Jonah. I have seen enough to make me sick; but if I faint in the day of adversity, my strength is small. I am under Mr Wesley's direction; and as he is father and friend, I hope I shall never turn my back on him.

Frank then paints a vivid picture of the new world, one that may have made quite an impression on those to whom the Asburys showed or read the letter:

"I have found at length that Americans are more willing to hear than to do; notwithstanding, there is a considerable work of God. We have had a large opening in Virginia and Maryland, where Mr Whitefield (an earlier visiting preacher) hardly had any success. The time to favour them I hope is come. Still old England for me.

"Yet this is a plentiful land; and if a poor man can live anywhere, he may live here. But my bread and water are sure, if I am faithful; and it is but little I want. I am not making a fortune, but to convert souls to God.

" 'Tis one great disadvantage to me I am not polite (NB: refined or cultured) enough for the people. They deem me fit for the country, but not for the cities; and it is my greater misfortune to cannot, or will not, learn, and they cannot teach me.

"But as my father and mother were never very polite people, it is not so strange. And as I was not born so, nor educated after this sort I cannot help it. Besides I was in the wilderness till my showing to Israel (NB: his conversion). But I see the emptiness of human life, and am sick of the gaudy scenes of life.

"I cannot as yet seek great things for myself, for I believe there will be, and is now, a dreadful consumption on earth among people who call themselves Christians because of their conformity to the world.

Frank then reminds his parents to give their hearts to God in order that they have a certainty they will meet in the kingdom of God. He urges them:

"Labour to support the preaching: it will not always be in vain. Stir up the people to meet together. Let me know if there is much spiritual prosperities in the societies about.

Frank then asks about a very practical matter:

"Let me know what is become of my mare.

Frank makes no mention in his Journal of writing his third surviving letter home dated September 5, 1773, evidently a busy Sunday in Baltimore cxxxviii. However he expresses disappointment at not having heard from them more often, or that they hadn't sent a letter through another preacher travelling from England. The letter also marks the moment that he ceased being "Frank" and began signing himself "Francis":

"My dear Parents,

"I long to hear oftener from you. I think I have had but two letters from you since I have been in America; but at such distance we must expect long returns. I am at present stationed in Maryland, and shall stay until Spring. Then, if the Lord spare me, I shall go to Virginia, and there continue until May, when our conference shall begin in Philadelphia.

"Mr Rankin told me he saw you, but I wonder you did not write. We the preachers and people in much order since the last to do here, as I am in the greatest part of the work, and we have many country born preachers and exhorters.

I bless God for health, I think better than ever; and I do feel my heart taken up with God and His work.

"When I consider the order and steadfastness of my own country friends, I wish almost to be with them. But I trust the time will come when I shall see them. Indeed, if I sought any thing but the glory of God, I should think this the only place in the world to answer my purpose. But God, that knows my heart, knoweth my desire is to spend and be spent in his service. I have had opportunities of pursuing fleshly ends, but I abhor them. Indeed we have a land of plenty. We can eat bread without scarceness."

Frank assures his parents that he continues to keep himself pure and trusts that they continue to seek holiness. He ends by referring to the shortness of the letter and again to the possibility that he may return to England:

"I am much taken up. Forgive the shortness of my letters. I have often to ride and preach twice in the daytime. My love to all friends. If I live, unless I should take a trip to the West Indies, I hope to be in England in less than two years.

"From your obedient and loving son, Francis Asbury" cxxxix.

During the War of Independence Frank had to lie low at various times, having to seek refuge with friends, one of whom was subsequently arrested for his pro-Methodist sympathies forcing Frank to seek another refuge.

cxxxviii *J&L Vol I p93.* cxxxix *J&L Vol III p17.*

Rival armies were crossing his mission field and there were very real dangers. On one occasion he came under fire when returning to Annapolis from a preaching appointment. One of his colleagues, Captain Thomas Webb, was arrested and accused of spying. Fellow preachers such as Webb, Shadford and Thomas Rankin gradually made their way back to England, and it is almost certain that news of Frank's difficulties and loyalties would filter back to Great Barr.

One of Frank's letters to a returning preacher, Thomas Rankin, was intercepted by the American forces. Frank had taken the opportunity to make clear his sympathy for the colonists and this enabled him to achieve greater trust, however, he never took American citizenship [cxl].

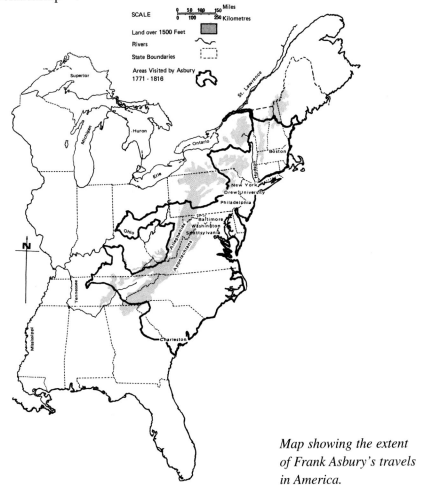

Map showing the extent of Frank Asbury's travels in America.

cxl *J&L Vol I p236-237; Vickers p19.*

13. Letters from America after the War

Relationships between the American colonies and the British government were becoming more strained. In April 1775 war broke out. Communications between Britain and America stopped altogether. Many of the British born preachers returned home, Wesley having made an ill judged attack on the colonists. Asbury chose to stay, often as a fugitive but with considerable sympathy for the newly emerging United States.

In 1783 Frank wrote to George Shadford, one of the preachers who had returned to England during the war, making clear his feelings about America, and probably his future, "O America! America! It certainly will be the glory of the world for religion! I have loved and do love America" [cxli].

It was not until Thursday May 20, 1784 that Frank, arriving at Baltimore for a conference, "learned by letter that my mother and father are yet alive". By this time they would be in their late sixties [cxlii], and Joseph was evidently unable to work.

The letters between the end of the war and Joseph's death are markedly different from those that survived from before the war. Frank was very concerned about his parents, knowing that neither was able to work.

Several themes come through. The difficulty of communicating over such great distances and the additional problems encountered in remitting small amounts of money. Frank's own financial situation was a great issue – he was clearly at pains to ensure his parents understood how little he was paid each year and how large a proportion of that he remitted home.

Sadly Frank was also anxious to counter some of the negative stories which were clearly being used in America by his opponents – that he was using profits from the sale of books and Methodist colleges to send great sums of money home.

It is obvious that Frank and his parents toyed with the idea that they should emigrate to America, something which Frank was clearly uncertain about, and in any case very hazardous for a couple over 60 years old.

Both Frank and his parents were heavily dependent on others to communicate. Frank made use of visiting preachers and friends from America such as Thomas Coke and George Suckley. Other families with sons in America, the Pirkins, the Foxalls, and the Smiths are those that we know of, would pass news about one another in their letters back to England, which would then be passed on. Frank was also writing to someone in Wednesbury, complaining to his parents on one occasion that he hadn't received a reply.

[cxli] *J&L Vol III p29.* [cxlii] *J&L Vol I p460.*

Eliza and Joseph had to rely on others too, such as Benjamin Rhodes and a Mr Phillips and a Mr Boon to write on their behalf.

These letters give a fascinating picture of Frank and his relationship with Eliza and Joseph. They are repetitious in places, possibly a precaution against them being lost en route. However they are reproduced here as fully as possible, as they are not easily available elsewhere.

During this period Eliza and Joseph would be hearing more and more of their son. It may not have occurred to them yet just how important he was in the development of Methodism in the new United States. Nor would they necessarily be able to grasp exactly how big the US may be, in their minds it may have the same stature as another English, but distant county, such as Cornwall or Northumberland.

1784

The conference at which he received his first letter for so many years had left him exhausted and a short break gave him the opportunity to reply in June 1784.

"My dear Parents:

"It gave me some comfort to hear of you, by the kind and friendly hand of Mr Boon, the first direct account I have received from you these seven years. My anxiety of mind would have been great for this; and my seeming disobedient absence, was I not sensible of superior obligations to my Heavenly Father, and reconciled God; to whom I go under all my exercises. I am perfectly happy in the circumstances I am under; believing the hand of God has been signally displayed, in bringing me to and preserving me in America.

"I find the judgement of our Revd. Friend and Father in God, Mr. Wesley, heartily concurs in my continuing here at present. What obligations are we under to that wonderful man of God! Oh how has my native land, and church, been favoured with a burning and shining light. What would thousands give, or do, could they but get him here. The esteem and influence I have among the preachers I owe much to him. We have upwards of eighty travelling preachers and near 15,000 members in society. Was I to leave America now, it would be against my own conviction that it is my duty to stay: and in this agrees the judgement of my friends on both sides of the water.

"You want to see me, I make no doubt, as I do you. My constitution is now remarkably seasoned to the country. I enjoy an uncommon share of health, under much labour of body and mind. I trust my dear parents, you have not wanted yet. In my travels I visit the parents of preachers, and think so will others do to mine."

Frank then raises the issue of money, having to use a fellow preacher as an intermediary to send such comparatively small amounts home. He explains his own circumstances and some of the difficulties he faced during the war.

"I sent a bill to Mr Sause of five pounds sterling, a few days ago. You should have received eleven guineas last autumn, by the same hand. You should be more particular in writing to me about these temporal matters. It is true you may be both disabled for labour, and may need a larger supply than I have given, or shall give; but we must trust Providence.

"Some say, was I to be paid according to my labour, my salary would be great. I can tell you how it has been with me from the first entering into the Connexion. I had to provide myself with necessary clothing and books. When I came to America, the first four or five years of my being here, money was plenty. With what I received more than bought me clothing (and I have been moderate in dress), I bought books. During the time of our late troubles, I sold my books, partly through want.

"My allowance from Conference is twenty four pounds currency, equal to twelve pounds sterling (or a little more, about $60) with my travelling expenses paid. I am concerned in the selling off the remains of Mr Wesley's and Williams' books. This puts money into my hands; but I know not that I can call my one coat and waistcoat, and half a dozen shirts, two horses and a few books, my own, if the debts were paid.

"'Tis true if I were to marry a wife with a fortune, or was less liberal, I might have more money. Many things have inclined me to continue in a single state. One, that once befell me in England. Another, my parents, - that if providence should open the way for me to come to you I may have no impediment; and that what I can save may go for your supply. Besides, my circuit is so large, not less than 700 miles in length yearly, and in circumstances I know not what."

Frank then discusses the possibility that both parents would come to him in America but quickly discounts the idea on grounds of expense, comfort and livelihood. He then writes directly to his mother, possibly quoting back part of her letter:

"You think 'could I see my child again, I should be happy, and die in peace.' Yes, if I could stay with you; but how painful to part. I am under some thought that America will be my country for life. If I ever had any ambition to be great, it is somewhat cooled; a less publick station would be more acceptable to me. A man may be suspected of pride and folly if he wants to rule.

"Upon the whole I have reason to praise God, who has kept me from publickly dishonouring him, His cause, the Connexion I am in, and the calling I am of; and to enjoy more of His power and love to my soul, that I am not puffed up nor fallen into the condemnation of the devil. What great reason I have to praise God for what is done, in, for, and by me; that a life of labour and suffering is my paradise, while love divine, transporting love, daily fills my heart.

"There is one thing that to me savours of human pride; and vanity, and expense (that is, to have my picture drawn) which I will have done if it would give you any satisfaction to send it to you; if it will remind you of me, and stir you up to pray that God may keep me; for there certainly never was a man of smaller abilities raised so high. I shall not wonder if some well meaning men should fear for me, this I do for myself."

Frank then gives a brief account of the recent conference before, once again, addressing his father's spiritual welfare:

"My dear father, cry to God for Grace to conquer sin. Take abundantly more care of your soul than your body. I pray for, think of, Oh that I could weep over, you more. May God restore you to his favour, and image and glory. Live in love together; ripen fast for glory; that there I may see and rejoice with you forever. If you desire my picture send the word in your next.

"I am as ever, your ever loving, tho' unworthy, Son, F Asbury" [cxliii].

Important changes were about to take place in the ministry of the Methodist Church in America and for Frank's status in life [cxliv].

The Anglican church collapsed during the American War of Independence. This denied the Methodist societies access to the sacraments of baptism and Holy Communion. John Wesley remedied the situation by himself ordaining Frank Asbury in absentia and Thomas Coke as joint superintendents together with Richard Whatcoat and

Thomas Vasey as elders. The service of ordination was performed by John Wesley assisted by Rev James Creighton in a house in Dighton Street, Bristol on September 1, 1784.

For Methodists in Britain, 1784 was a year of controversy and change. Gradually most Methodists were realising that they would eventually become a separate church, but Wesley was very reluctant to formally break away. The Methodists in America were forced by circumstance rather than theology to confront the issue earlier than their British brothers and sisters.

Armed with Wesley's letter to "Our Brethren in America" [cxlv] Coke, Whatcoat and Vasey set out for America in order to ordain

Thomas Vasey.

[cxliii] *J&L Vol III p37.* [cxliv] *J.A. Vickers p20-22.* [cxlv] *J&L Vol III p37.*

Asbury. Twelve days before his ordination at the Baltimore Christmas Conference, Frank wrote home, his parents had evidently made it clear that they were unhappy with him writing to others more often than he wrote to them and he responded in a postscript.

"My dear Father and Mother:

I write a few lines to let you know I am in health. My soul more than ever waits for God and is filled with zeal for his glory. I have seen the lightening down of the power of the Lord and expect to see greater things yet.

"I was thankful to God that I heard of your welfare by Brother Whatcoat who is safe arrived to help us. I was made joyful above measure at the arrival of our British Brethren. We are greatly rejoiced that if we are not worthy to have Mr Wesley (whom our Preachers and people venerate if possible, more that the Europeans), we are favoured with the man of his right hand, Dear Dr. Coke, - if only for a few months.

"I hope you cleave to God wholly, and are in great earnest about your souls. Oh may you ripen fast for glory! This is the wish and daily prayers of your unworthy son, and souls real friend, F. Asbury

"PS I hope to send a little supply about Christmas, in an order to Mr Atlay, London. Hearing it is a matter of grief to you for me to write to others and not to you I shall write often and short" cxlvi.

1785

Thomas Coke returned to England soon afterwards and visited the Birmingham area, possibly carrying a lost letter on behalf of Frank to his parents. News of their activities in America were gaining attention in England.

The local newspaper the Aris Birmingham Gazette carried the following reports:

"By the latest accounts from America we learn that a college is building at Abingdon, in Hartford County, Maryland: The presentation to which is to be in the Principal members and friends of the Methodist Episcopal Church. The plan is by the Rev. Dr. Coke, a Devonshire Clergyman, and Mr Francis Asbury, of the neighbourhood of Birmingham, both esteemed preachers among the Methodists who a few years ago went over to America with many other gentlemen to propagate the gospel among the Indians in that part of the globe." (23 May 1785 No 2271)

"On Sunday 12 inst in the afternoon, a most excellent sermon was preached in the Rev Mr Wesley's chapel in this town, by the Rev Mr Coke LLD, lately arrived from

cxlvi *J&L Vol III p39.*

America, after which a collection was made for Kingswood School near Bristol which amounted to £16.18s 8d" (25 July 1785 No 2280).

1786

Frank's next surviving letter was written on Saturday January 14, 1786. He had arrived in Charlestown, South Carolina the previous day, but was unwell and another preacher took his place. There is no entry in his Journal for the Saturday, although the following Sunday was back in the pulpit [cxlvii]. On this unscheduled day of inactivity Frank wrote to his parents:

"My dear Parents,

"If Providence will so dispose of us that we shall not see each other in time, let us live for eternity, and labour to meet in Glory. I comfort myself that while Doctor Coke lives, and remains in England, I shall insure you a friend. O that you would each of you live to God, and press after holiness; that your title and qualification for heaven may be good.

"I enjoy great health for this climate, and my labours. I love my European friends. I cannot write to them all; but salute them in the Lord. At the earnest request of the Doctor, and for Mr Wesley's Magazine, I have been at the trouble to have my picture drawn. I intend to send it to the Doctor to be engraved, and then to be returned to you. I should have thought this high vanity in me, had it not been done on these considerations.

"Remember for many years, I lived with, and laboured, and prayed for you. I at this distance of time, and place, care for, and send to your relief, and cease not night and day to pray for you, who am as ever your most unworthy, but dutiful son in the Lord, Francis Asbury" [cxlviii].

Whether the Eliza and Joseph ever received the original drawing intended for the Arminian Magazine we do not know. They certainly didn't see it in the magazine, as no engraving appeared until, 1809!

1788

During the next two years Frank Asbury and Thomas Coke's title gradually changed from being "Superintendent" of the Methodist Episcopal Church of America, to that of "Bishop". This did not please John Wesley and in 1788 he wrote a stern letter to "Frankey" expressing his displeasure [cxlix]. Whether Eliza and Joseph were aware of the new title or of Wesley's objections we do not know.

[cxlvii] *J&L Vol I p506.* [cxlviii] *J&L Vol III p46-47.* [cxlix] *J&L Vol III p64-65.*

Wesley's magazine The Arminian carried a very full account of the growth of the Methodist Church in America introduced by Thomas Coke. "In some parts of Virginia the congregation on Sabbath Days consists of several thousand", says one of several excited items. The articles refer to several preachers including John Dickins, Hope Hull, and James O'Kelly, who was later to have lead a bitter dispute with Frank. Curiously there is no mention of Frank [cl].

1790

Frank however had other worries concerning his parents and his next surviving letter, written from Charleston, South Carolina on Sunday February 14, 1790 shows that he was hearing of their welfare through Thomas Coke:

"My dear Parents

"My mind is at rest with respect to your temporalities, from the assurance I have had that brother Coke will supply you at my desire. O that your souls may grow in grace and that you may make sure work for eternity. My head and hands and heart are full. Being so continually on the stretch in travelling, I have little time to write to my dearest friends.

"Glory be to the LORD, we have a glorious work. Hundreds are coming home to God: - east, west, north and south. I praise God I ever was born to see the glory of God in the new world. My dear – children, and their children, the poor Indians, are the subjects of my charge. If God's people throughout the world would begin to pray for and strive to believe that the Lord would awaken thousands, it would soon appear in every town, country, parish, house and individual.

"O that God may make his power known in my poor native land, and break like thunder and lightning on the people that have long been sleeping in the form of sentiments of religion.

"I am not pleased at our Wednesbury friends, if they have received my letter, for not writing. I wish you would get some person to write to me, a large satisfactory account. Where is aunt Sarah Rogers? Where is uncle Nathaniel Rogers? Where is his son John Rogers? Where, what, is Joseph Groves? Tell me the whole.

"I am as ever, your dear son, F. Asbury [cli].

In 1790 the first mention of Frank's name occurred in the Arminian Magazine when George Shadford, one of the British preachers who went to America shortly after Frank, explained how he came to leave America and part from Frank. It is highly likely that

[cl] *The Arminian Magazine September 1788.* [cli] *J&L Vol III p85.*

Eliza and Joseph had already heard this story for themselves either directly from Shadford or through word and mouth from other Methodists.

"..I said to Brother Asbury 'let us have a day of fasting and prayer, that the Lord may direct us; for we never were in such circumstances as now since we are both Methodist Preachers.' We did so, and in the evening, I asked him how he found his mind? He said, he did not see his way clear to go to England. I told him I could not stay, as I believed I had done my work here at present; and that it was much impressed, upon my mind to go home now as it had been to come over to America. He replied, "Then one of us must be under a delusion." I said "Not so; I may have a call to go and you to stay," and I believed we both obeyed the call of Providence. We saw we must part, though we loved one another as David and Jonathan.

George Shadford.

1791

A lengthy report on a journey through New Jersey written by Frank to John Wesley in September 1783 appeared in the Arminian Magazine clii.

This was also the year of John Wesley's death and soon afterwards the British Methodists were engulfed in controversy as some sought to establish Methodism as an entirely distinct church from the Church of England. In Barr and West Bromwich this led to Asbury's lifelong friend Thomas Ault leaving the Methodist Society as he remained a "Church Methodist" rather than supporting the "New Plan".

1792

Frank was clearly becoming very well known. Samuel Taylor a visiting preacher recorded in his diary:

'Preached at Barr, a village famous for nothing as having given birth to
Mr Francis Asbury of America and being the present residence of his parents, at whose house we preached' 11 June 1792' cliii.

clii *The Arminian Magazine July 1791.* cliii *PWHS Vol XX11 p121.*

1793

During the next few years George Suckley came to play an important part in the relationship between Frank and his parents. Suckley also became a firm friend of Frank and offered him accommodation when in New York. It was to the Suckley family that Frank presented the portrait of his mother for safekeeping, which he requested in 1798. Suckley was an English Methodist who came to New York with Thomas Coke. He established himself as a successful merchant and apparently travelled between New York and the English West Midlands on business.

In late August 1793 Frank arrived in New York for a conference. He had been feeling unwell for the previous four months. A few days earlier he had had a fall from his horse that had left him lame. Frank was evidently a little depressed about his preaching of the doctrine of sanctification and was resolving to preach more pointedly. New York was very hot and infected with fevers and influenza which Frank caught. During his confinement, possibly at the Suckley house, he took the opportunity to write home [cliv]:

"My ever dear Parents:

I am pleased to hear by Mr Suckley, (who was at the house), of your welfare. I expect by this time brother Sause has supplied you with a small sum of money. I shall not forget to supply you in future. It is but once a year that I visit our cities and sea-ports. I am called in a very peculiar manner to help in the planting of the Gospel westward.

"O what you have to do now but to spend half your time in meditation and prayer; to make your last days by far your best. I know not how you feel. But, although I have not seen fifty years, I feel many infirmities, but Christ is all and in all.

"I am resolved to give myself wholly to God, through my short day. I trust not only thousands annually join us, but 3000 are converted to God every year. I wish I would desire Mr Taylor, or someone, to write to me once in three or six months. Mrs Smith's son was with me this morning. I shall try to put forward to something, if in my power.

"My love to all my friends, Francis Asbury"

Frank then added to following notes on the preceding letter:

"I have the flower of my days in hearing and speaking for God and Christ. It is now near thirty years I have been speaking. I cannot, as heretofore, preach fifteen or sixteen times in seven days. I thank God for the use of my eyes, and ears, and tongue. I often pray for

[cliv] *J&L Vol I p769.*

you. O that my parents may be saved from all sin before they die, that I may have the best assurance of your going to glory.

"I think it would be best for you to sell any useless property you have, and live upon the proceeds. I shall never want or possess anything you have. I do most earnestly wish, if my mother should outlive my father, she would come to see me, if able, and I am alive. I greatly rejoice that the seed of Methodism sown by me in Great Barr, groweth. I congratulate the society.

"Two and twenty years have greatly defaced features and families out of my remembrance. It is no matter. We shall hereafter know better than we are now known. I trust you will cry to God for the souls around you, that awakenings and conversions to God may be frequent amongst you, and believers may be sanctified. The Lord can work like himself.

"O for a constant, pure, heavenly flame! I trust and hope the Lord has converted two or three thousand souls in the United States the last year. We have about 300 zealous travelling preachers, and near 700 local. We have the range of fourteen or fifteen states like small kingdoms; indeed some like large ones, the whole continent 1,400 miles from north to south and a thousand from east to west. I have not forgotten Old England, although I never wish to reside there. Yet, I could wish to visit it for only 8 or 10 months.

"I am your very dear, F. Asbury." [clv].

1794

This would have been the year when Frank's achievement would have been obvious for all in England to see.

Freeborn Garrettson, an early American companion, and by then a leading Methodist preacher had his life story serialised in the Arminian Magazine. The January edition set the tone for what was to follow in the following months. He wrote "...Mr Francis Asbury came into our County. I went to hear him one evening. The place was much crowded, however I got to the door and listened with attention. The sound was sweeter than honey, or the honey comb. I could have tarried there to the rising sun."

The Arminian also carried a table showing the sheer size of the Methodist Church in America with 66,191 members both black and white with the Bishops Frank Asbury and Thomas Coke pointedly listed as "superintendents" [clvi].

That same year the Minutes of Conference showed that the British Church numbered 75,052 [clvii].

[clv] *J&L Vol III p121-122.* [clvi] *The Arminian Magazine 1794, p200-204.* [clvii] *Minutes of Conference 1794 p283.*

Despite this fame and recognition, in an undated letter, but probably written from Philadelphia in June 1794, Frank expresses his pain that his parents had written to tell him, and others had told him, that money sent to them by Frank had failed to arrive. His parents were now approaching 80 years old and he would certainly have been alarmed to hear of their plight. He reassures them that he had made an arrangement with Richard Whatcoat, an old friend from the Wednesbury society and with him in America to care for them in the event of his death.

Sadly again he has to defend himself from those trying to blacken his name, arguing that he was using the profits from the Methodist publishing ventures to send money home:

"My very dear Father and Mother,

"I have had some considerable pain of mind from two or three letters I have received from you, as also the information given by others, that the money was not paid. I have certain information that Mr.———— received a sum last September, or thereabout. I last evening made an arrangement for a remittance to you, by my agent John Dickens, with Mr Suckley, the young man who made you a visit last year. It will come by Mr Holley, transmitted to Mr James Foster, in Birmingham. This sum will come into your hands in the space of three or four months. There will be a great certainty of this cash coming into your hands.

"My salary is fourteen pounds, ten shillings sterling ($64). I have sold my watch and library, and would sell my shirts before you should want. I have made a reserve for you. I spend very little on myself. My friends find me some clothing. I might have money, but the wicked world, and those that leave our connexion, strive to blacken my character by saying I have profits of books at my command, and profits from the College, and schools established in many parts of America.

"These reports I am able to refute, and yet they say 'he remits money to his parents every year.' The contents of a small saddle bag will do for me, and one coat in the year. Your son, Francis, is a man of honour and conscience. As my father and mother never disgraced me with an act of dishonesty, I hope to echo back the same sound of an honest, upright man.

"I wish to despise flattery and injustice. I hope you will guard against fretfulness and discontent. I am well satisfied that the Lord saw fit you should be my parents, rather than the king and queen, or any of the great; also, as to when and where I drew my breath. I sometimes think you will outlive me. I have made my will, and left my all to you, and that's soon done. While I live and do well I will remember you every year;

perhaps come to see you, if you live many years, and peace and harmony should take place between the continent and the kingdom.

"I rejoice that religion prospers once more in my native land. Above all, my dear father and mother, seek a deeper sense of God and religion, to be holy and ripe for glory. O that your last days may be your best! And that you may not only live long, but live and die well.

"Only be much in prayer, that your day of grace may never be past, while life and thought and being last to all eternity. I am much obliged to those kind brethren that have written to me on your behalf. I beg you will take every opportunity of writing to me your true state of body and mind! If I should be removed, I have left the charge with brother Whatcoat to do for you in my place.

"I am as ever, your dear son, Francis Asbury" clviii.

The following September at the start of the 1794 conference Frank took the opportunity of writing home, possibly because he had received a letter from his parents or others in England:

"My very dear Father and Mother,

"I am not unmindful of your present and eternal welfare. When I was in Philadelphia, in July, I remembered you; and I hope by this time you feel the effects of my filial duty. I desire I may hear from you all the particulars of your souls and bodies. I wish to know who among the poor old neighbours are converted to the Lord, and live religion. I suspect, were I to return, I should be a stranger in the place where I was born.

"I am at present in a good state of health. Time has been when I feared I should leave the world before my poor parents, and you would come to want. But God is all sufficient. The earth is the Lord's and the fullness thereof.

"O let me hear, if you go hence, that you die triumphant in the Lord, and go shouting to glory. We are not without the down pourings of the Spirit of God in a wonderful manner. But I want the continent, the world, to flame with the spiritual glory of God.

"O my father! O my mother! Be much in prayer for meek, patient, loving, holy souls. O how awful to live almost one hundred years and not be fit for heaven and glory.

"I am, as ever, your dear, faithful obedient son, F. Asbury" clix.

---

clviii *J&L Vol III p127-128.* clix *J&L Vol III p130.*

1795

Just a year later in October 1795 the difficulties of sending money home were again pressing on Frank and his parents. A day of rest following another conference was taken up with writing another letter home:

"My very dear Parents,

"I am pleased to hear from you, by Benjamin Rhodes, or any other person. I am sorry you had not what I mentioned in my last. I wrote to you a few weeks back, from Philadelphia. I have delivered into the hands of my book agent the supply for the present year. By a late letter I am informed it will soon be transmitted to you. Were it ten thousand per year, if I had it in my possession, you should be more than welcome, if you had need of it.

"No person could have been in more difficult circumstances than myself. It is wickedly reported of me that I collect money from the printing concern and college, and send it home to my friends, in large sums. This is done by wicked men whom I have prevented from oppressing and robbing the Church of God. To cover their own basement they charge me; so that my good to you is evil spoken of.

"I hope you use carefully what I dearly purchase by riding six or seven thousand miles a year, besides sitting in and conducting conferences of two hundred preachers, and the charge of many things for the cause of Christ. The coat and waistcoat I now have on I have worn thirteen months, and I would not carry a second shirt if I could do without it.

"But all these things are but trifles. If you are wholly given up to God, the Gospel is preached to my poor neighbours and their children, I shall rejoice.

"I have enjoyed great health, and have travelled extensively through twelve of the United States, now growing into little kingdoms. I had hopes of seeing you, but now they fail, unless you come to me. My one prevailing desire is that you may make sure work for heaven.

I am often thankful you have kept open house for the word and people of God, almost forty years. Go on, my dear parents. You hear so often from me that you will think you see me, and I am very near you. Never give your souls a moments uneasiness about living. If I live and do well in temporals, you shall live also.

"Think not that anything comes grudgingly from me. Could you eat wedges of gold, if I had them you should be welcome to them.

"I should be glad if you could take the time of my baptism from the church register, that I may know it perfectly. It will cost you but a shilling, unless that, as everything else, is doubled.

"Provisions are high with us; but workmen's wages are in proportion. Four shillings and sixpence a day labourer's wages in summer; and in towns common labourers gain that always. I am as ever you most unworthy, yet most obedient, loving son, F. Asbury" [clx].

1796

Shortly afterwards, possibly in December 1795 or January 1796 when at Charleston, South Carolina, Frank wrote a reply to his parents, obviously upset about the difficulties of maintaining communication and ensuring that they were receiving financial support.

He urges them to contact Thomas Coke for assistance which Frank will then repay. He also rules out again any possibility of them travelling to the United States. Finally he makes it clear he has to forget his own country and his "father's house". By this time Frank believes he is writing up to one thousand letters a year [clxi] and it is possible that the pressures of maintaining such a flow of letters whilst constantly on the move showed in his letters home:

"My very dear Parents,

"It is with great difficulty I can communicate to your wants, or even be informed of them. I have requested and will request Doctor Coke, as he is so frequently in England, to know and supply, or order a supply of all your wants.

"Every act of kindness done to you in England, I shall return to the Doctor when in America; and also repay what he requires. I am in great straits about advising you to come hither. It would be attended with great expense and danger; and should you suffer, by land or water, it would give me great pain.

"My hands are very full, I am here, and there, and everywhere, upon the continent. But I should fear nothing so much as your not being devoted to God, or so holy as you ought to be.

"I frequently pray for you. I want to see you both in heaven; it is but a little, yea, a very little time, and we shall close our concerns here. If at any time you be shortened, write to the Doctor, and he will supply you, and I will answer him.

"If I were not about a great work, and under indispensable obligations to the preachers and people here, chiefly raised up under my ministry, you might hope to see me. I have reason to believe, and that firmly, that the hand of God has been clearly seen in bringing me to, and continuing me in this land, from the first moment to the present.

[clx] *J&L Vol III134-135.* [clxi] *J&L Vol II p76.*

"We have opened a house for learning. So far I am concerned for the present and rising generation. I am in some measure, constrained to forget my own country, and my father's house. I am as ever, your affectionate son, F. Asbury" clxii.

Arriving in Philadelphia in July 1796 Frank was delighted to hear that his friend George Suckley was about to go to England. Frank took the opportunity to write a letter and send money to his parents which seemed noticeably more relaxed than those previously sent in recent years. There is no journal entry for the day, July 29 clxiii and it seems that Frank spent the day reading and writing, but with constant interruptions:

"My very dear and never to be forgotten Parents,

"I came providentially to this city, and had hardly time to breathe, after reading several momentous letters, from various parts of our continent, when I was told Mr Suckley was going to England. I hope to embrace this opportunity of sending you what little I have saved since my last remembrance of you.

"I wrote to you from Charleston. Perhaps I was constrained from the high sense of filial duty I had, to invite you here. I feared England would be in blood. I now think you are much better where you are. And I sincerely wish I could come to you, but I see no way without sinning against God, and the Church.

"Since I wrote from Charleston, I have travelled nearly two thousand five hundred miles, through Georgia, South and North Carolina, and Virginia, Maryland and Delaware. Hard wear, and hard fare. But I am healthy and lean, grey headed and dim sighted. But I hope I enjoy as much of religion, or more than ever, preaching, living and feeling.

"I wrote to Doctor Coke to let you have ten guineas, and would repay him when he comes to the continent. I must watch every opportunity to send you small sums. As my life is an uncertainty, I have employed a person to transcribe my journals for the press; either here, or in England.

"You know how long I served the church for nothing. I might if I would, have money; but I am set for the defence of the Gospel. When man will labour as hard for God, as for man, and take no more than poor men ought to have, God will own them.

"O my dear father and mother, be wholly for God! Make haste to get ready for glory! I have great cause to mourn over my dear America! The people are growing wealthy and wicked. It is not with our society as we could wish.

"I wish you to take care to write to me often as you can. I am not sure what I shall remit. Mr Suckley is my very great and kind friend, and yours also. Whatever I send, he will faithfully apply to your service.

clxii *J&L Vol III p137.* clxiii *J&L Vol II p92.*

"I am now returning from a journey of about three thousand five hundred miles, since the beginning of November 1795, to this date. I now commend you to God. As ever, your dear and only son, Francis Asbury.

PS: I am now, in the heat of our season, going to New England, which is Old England continued. I shall pass through New Jersey, the state of New York, Connecticut, and Massachusetts; performing perhaps, a tour of near one thousand miles, before I come back to Baltimore which is like my centre and my home. It may be happy for me, let the climate be healthy or unhealthy, to soul or body, hard or easy: I soon change. You will excuse my manner of writing. I have been called off several times since I began this epistle" clxiv.

Shortly before his fifty first birthday, which would be August 1796, Frank wrote again to his parents. Once again he had evidently received a batch of letters apparently asking him to return home, an issue he hadn't addressed in the letter sent with George Suckley just a few weeks earlier. The writer of one of the letters on his parents' behalf, Brother Rhodes, is apparently seeking a business opportunity, and it seems that Frank is again open to the idea that his parents should join him in America:

"My own dear Father and Mother:

"I have received several letters expressive of your paternal love and gratitude towards me. I have often revolved the serious thought of my return to you. To say nothing of the State of Europe, and Britain, or the society, with whom I claim, in England. I have frequently asked myself, can you retire to a single circuit, and act as a lay preacher, and step down?

"This is not my difficulty, if I know my own heart. With humility and self-abasement I may say, one hundred thousand respectable citizens of the New World, and 300 travelling and 600 local brethren, would advise me not to go. I hope the voice of the people is the voice of God. At present we have more work, than faithful workmen. We have a state or two out of 17 states and territories, that call for help, and we are not able to supply or support it.

"I am like Joseph, I want to have you near me. I am not ashamed of your poverty; and I after so many years professing religion, you will not be wanting in piety. I have considered you have that which is my joy and glory; that you have opened doors above 40 years for religious exercise, when no other would or even dared to do it. It is a serious subject whether you think it is your duty still to keep a place for preaching, or if upon your removal the Gospel will be taken from poor Barr!

clxiv J&L Vol III p142-143.

"Yet when I think you have no child, nor friends that careth for you, the distress of the land, and the high price of provisions, I wish to see you, and have you near me. 'Tis true, whilst I live you will live also; if I keep my place and piety.

"I have passed the slippery paths of youth; and am now entering the 51st year of my life, I have very different views and feelings. I have had the burden of a school, hastily called a college, by Dr. Coke. I gave that up into the hands of trustees made by law. I study daily, what I can do without one horse, and that sometimes borrowed, one cloak, one great coat, one waistcoat, (the last coat and waistcoat I used about 14 months), 4 or 5 shirts, 4 or 5 books.

"I am in doubt that if I should be called away you will not be provided for so well as among those I have faithfully laboured for this 24 years. It is true you are not immortal, anymore than myself, judging according to the nature of things you may go first, one or both of you. All these things I have weighed in my mind. I wish you reconsider the matter, and ask much counsel of God, and your best and most impartial friends.

"I have received information of thirty guineas put into the hands of Mr Suckley, to remit to your service. I received a letter from Brother Rhodes on your behalf, for which I am much obliged to him. On the subject he wrote to me, let him know I avoid all worldly encumbrances. Our book interest is in the hands of John Dickins, in Philadelphia. Brother Dickins keepeth a stationers shop. Should he choose to receive his grammars in sheets without the British constitution, he may safely send them. The Americans think their own constitution the best. John Hagerty, in Baltimore, keepeth a stationery. He may trade with him also. Should the grammars come over by our General Conference, the preachers may take some.

"I shall remember you by Dr Coke. I wish my dear parents to consider the matter and send me another letter between this and the 20th October (NB date of next General Conference which Dr Coke would attend). Whether I be present or absent, dead, or alive, I trust my friends in Baltimore will take care of you, by my help.

"You have spent many pounds upon Christian people, I know from my childhood. Happy I was when this was done; and I hope it will come home to you in mercy. You must make it a matter of much fasting, and prayer, before you attempt anything. You must not expect to see me above once a year. I hope the accounts I have had of the piety of you both are not too large. May you ripen fast for glory.

"We have not any extraordinary displays of the power of God. America is the young child of God and providence, set upon the lap, dandled upon the knees, prest to the consoling mercies. But we are not as thankful as we ought to be. The salvation of the church I wish to make the cause of my life. I stand in such a situation, and relation for the state of the ministry and people. I may have a thousand letters a year, while swiftly moving through the continent every year.

"The time certainly is drawing near when universal peace shall bless the earth: when distracted Europe, superstitious Asia, blind Africa, and America shall more abundantly see the salvation of our God. Oh let us be much in prayer. For the health of my body and by the desire of my friends, I stop two months, in the soft climate of Charleston, South Carolina, the winter months. To avoid the rains. It is supposed my complaints have been derived from changes of lodging, and weather. I must travel rapidly for 10 months.

"My kind love to Brother Rhodes. I remember well seeing him at Witney, and his giving his horses something when sick. I am as ever your unworthy but loving son F. Asbury" clxv.

In June 1797 Frank recorded in his diary that a portrait artist from Birmingham, Thomas Barber, visited him in Baltimore to paint a second likeness at the request of Eliza. Thomas Barber had arrived in Baltimore with his wife Ester in 1794. He died in 1797 clxvi. He was not the celebrated portrait painter also called Thomas Barber from Nottingham nor related as far as can be known to Joseph Vincent Barber in Birmingham, another well known artist and teacher.

The two sittings were apparently at different locations. One sitting was at the home of a Mr Hawkins clxvii the other at the home of Moses Hand, also a portrait painter.

Eliza received two portraits of Frank, one for herself and the other for the superintendent of the Wednesbury circuit. The one from the cottage was eventually hung at the school house at Snails Green where Mrs Moseley, the wife of the schoolmaster, a relative of the Asburys lived clxviii. One of these Barber portraits, donated by the Hands family, is now exhibited in the main reading room of the Lovely Lane Methodist Museum in Baltimore clxix.

Portrait of Francis Asbury which was sent home to England.

---

clxv *J&L Vol III p144-146.* clxvi *Email from Suni K Johnson, Lovely Lane Museum 17/01/03.* clxvii *J&L Vol II p129n.* clxviii *Joseph Reeves, MWHSB. Vol 1 p11-12.* clxix *Email from Suni Johnson as above.*

1797

In November 1797 Frank was in Virginia with Thomas Coke. He had recently picked up two letters from his parents and wrote what he described as "a short pathetic letter to my parents" clxx. Once again he reiterates that he intends to stay in America. It was the last surviving letter addressed to both parents:

"My very dear, and never to be forgotten Father and Mother:

"I have received your letters, written in 1795 and 1796, and must wish you to get some friends to write very circumstantially once a year. I have been laying by, in the hands of our general book steward, in Philadelphia about twenty guineas. The distance, and the difficulties of remitting money are great, at least in such small sums. I have now resolved that the only way will be for our general book steward to send his orders to Mr George Whitefield in London.

"I have strong assurances of brethren on both sides of the water that they will take care of you, if I were dead. But all flesh is grass! It is with the greatest difficulty I can see you supplied while in life; and as much whisper and noise about it as though I had sent you thousands. How will it be when I am gone to rest! Next to leaving the church, I feel for you. We must learn, you and I, to trust God.

"It gives me pleasure to think you have kept open house for near forty years, and spent what you had to spare on the cause of God. I hope my dear neighbours, and the rising generations, will not forget to praise God, and remember the name Asbury, that brought and supported the Gospel among them.

"If I were to leave America I should break my heart; and if I stay perhaps I shall break my constitution. But here I must die! May you find a safe passage from England, and I from America, to glory.

"I send a small present for each. I have settled with Doctor Coke for the ten pounds. If the Doctor should offer you money you may take it, I shall use every prudential means to pay him. I must now, as I have done this thirty and eight years, commend you to God, and remain your unworthy, yet grateful son, F. Asbury" clxxi.

Three days later he wrote to Alexander Mather clxxii, one of those who helped in those early days of faith in the Wednesbury society.

---

clxx *J&L Vol II p140.* clxxi *J&L Vol III p166-167.* clxxii *as note 154 above.*

14. Letters and Life after Joseph

Frank first heard his father was seriously ill and close to death on June 3, 1798, when in Philadelphia [clxxiii]. In fact Joseph was already dead and had been buried at St Margaret's churchyard on 17 March. He immediately wrote to Eliza:

"My dear Mother,

"From information I have received, I fear my venerable father is no more an inhabitant of this earth; you a widow, myself an orphan, with respect to a father. I cannot tell how to advise you in this important change. I dare not forbid your coming to this continent.

"At present, I have neither health, nor purse, nor inclination, nor confidence, to re-cross the seas. It was there my serious times began. Comparatively I never knew change or trouble till I became an inhabitant of the sea; and in the new world. You have washed the saints' feet this forty years; you have entertained strangers, brought up children, and have done some good works.

"It is a comfort to my soul when I reflect that you have kept the Gospel ministry in your house for so many years, whilst, with my small abilities, I have been doing a little to spread the Gospel through sixteen states, any one of them, except two, affording more space than England. I wish you to stay, to support the cause of Christ in your house, to the latest hour.

"If my father is taken away, I advise you to take a pious prudent woman to live with you, for company, and consolation. If I should wear my coat, one of the kind, with other parts of the apparel, fourteen or fifteen months, I will try to remit as heretofore. I have formed no other connection. This might give you some assurance that I am still your son.

"As to the reward for the troubles you have felt, what compensation can I give? It is pretty well known here that I was born poor, my calling and everything. We have had many who have risen up from Europe, and in this country, that could not have their gratification, and have cast at me what they could find. I thank my God, I have been able to live up, in some degree, to the dignity and duty of a Christian and a minister.

"I am exceedingly pleased with the attention Mr Phillips has paid and will pay to you. You have had yourself respectable, and extensive in friends, who, although they cannot give to you, can comfort you. I have been, as you may already have heard,

[clxxiii] *J&L Vol II p160.*

77

afflicted by excessive labours of mind and body. I had to neglect writing, reading, and preaching, for a time. I only attempt to preach on Sabbath days. I have had many ounces of blood taken away.

"I had to stop and lie by in some precious families, where parents and children, in some measure, supplied your absence. I laid by in Virginia. When you hear the name, you will love it unseen, and say, 'That this is where my Frank was sick'. I am much mended, and live wholly upon a vegetable diet.

"I move in a little carriage, being unable to ride upon horseback. My route ought to be three thousand miles a year. I should wish, if a few guineas would procure it, a perfect plain portrait of yourself. O my mother! Let us be holy, and watch, and pray, that we may meet in heaven. You have professed religion fifty years, living, feeling religion; a mother you ought to be in Israel.

"Your numerous friends will hear, and listen, when you die, to know if your last days were peace and triumph! Were you to see me, and the colour of your hair, nearly that of your own. But still God is with me. My soul exults in God. As ever, your dear son, Francis Asbury" [clxxiv].

A few days later a letter arrived from Mr Philips, confirming Joseph's death [clxxv].

It was a year before Frank heard directly from Eliza. He was attending conferences in and New York state, [clxxvi] and his correspondence caught up with him:

"My very dear Mother,

"I have received yours dated in the years 1798 and 1799, both in the same week. Letters coming to me are landed at one end of the continent, when I am at the other, and are sent after me; but before they arrive, I am gone. I am thankful to God that my dear father died in peace; and that my mother yet lives, to serve God, and his ministers and people.

"I gladly consent to your refusal to come to America. You might find yourself disappointed, as many have done, in coming to this continent. If my way were open to return, my difficulties would be great, in crossing the seas at this time of general distress of nations, the sea and the waves roaring, men's hearts failing them for fear of those things which shall come upon the earth, when nations are destroying each other by thousands in a day, if not an hour. I am satisfied in your living alone, if you have such kind and watchful neighbours. My love and kind respects to them, for their attention to you.

"The coming of Christ is near, even at the door, when he will establish his kingdom. He is now sweeping the earth, to plant it with righteousness and true

[clxxiv] *J&L Vol III p169-171.* [clxxv] *J&L Vol II p163.* [clxxvi] *J&L Vol II 196.*

holiness. My eyes are weak enough, even with glasses. When I was a child, and would pry into the Bible by twinkling fire light, you used to say 'Frankey, you will spoil your eyes.' At that time I sought the historical letter. I knew not the hidden pure light and life. It is my grief that I cannot preach as heretofore. I am greatly worn out at fifty five; but it is a good cause.

"I am as ever, your dear son in the Gospel, Francis Asbury" [clxxvii]

Within a few weeks or months, the letter is undated, Frank wrote again to his mother briefly telling her that he intended sending her another 30 guineas. He also seems keen to reassure her of his good health. This appears to be the last surviving letter Frank sent home whilst she was still alive:

"My most dearly beloved Mother:

"I am yet living, with a restoration of health, to continue to labour and travel, night and day. I am, of late, more than ever invigorated, with a revival of religion in various happy parts of our continental field. Whilst wars and want prevail (in other places), we have peace and religion. I have not time to write at large. I hope to manifest my duty and care, by sending you thirty guineas. You will please to let me know if this supply is sufficient. I am not in cash at present, but trust I shall be in a few weeks.

"I remain as ever, your affectionate son, Francis Asbury" [clxxviii].

During the week of January 20th 1800 Frank was in Charleston and was suffering from a bowel complaint for which he was prescribed a concoction of bark, rhubarb and nutmeg, which helped him. He used the opportunity to reply to correspondents in Maine, Massachusetts, New York, Jersey, Pennsylvania and Virginia. He doesn't record in his journal that he also wrote home to his mother [clxxix].

Just one letter of Eliza to survives, many were believed lost in a fire at the Methodist Printing House in 1904. It was in reply to a letter Frank had written whilst in Charleston. The reply had been written on her behalf by Sam Barkley, the local preacher.

There is one rather puzzling comment. She says "I live in Richard Longmore's house; and have lived there about twenty years." Whether this means she had a lodger or he was her landlord we cannot tell from the official transcription. A later American visitor apparently met those "who lived in the cottage and took care of the old people until they died" [clxxx].

[clxxvii] *J&L Vol III 181.* [clxxviii] *J&L Vol III p182-183.* [clxxix] *J&L Vol II p223.* [clxxx] *Fisk p606.*

Eliza's letter brings Frank up to date with many of the names mentioned elsewhere:

"My very dear Son:

"May Israel's God (whose you are, and whom you love) bless you in body, soul and labours, Amen. Your welcome letter from Charles-Town, South Carolina, dated January 21 came duly to hand, and found me very poorly. My legs swelled much, and I was very sick and faint: and I began to think my Heavenly Father was about to call me home, and I bless His holy Name I was quite resigned to His blessed will to go home, unless He saw that by staying a little longer, I could promote his glory.

"However through Mercy, I am now much better. I can wear my own shoes, and go about again, only the affliction has left me weaker than I was; but I trust that I shall get a little more strength.

"I rejoice that the Lord has supported you as He has, these many years. It is not to be wondered at, that you find some infirmities after so much and so long labour and fatigue. However, you are still in good hands, and the great head of the church will dispose of you to His glory.

"Should you see your native land before I am removed: you may well think, I should rejoice to embrace you. But this I leave with Him who cannot err. I sincerely thank you for your care toward me. What you sent for my support last year, duly came to hand.

"Your Aunt Sarah Rogers has been dead some time. I am glad the good work is going on in that New World. You began to meet the people at Sutton in July 1764. You was born in August 1745.

"I am glad that Joseph Pirkins is doing well in temporals: may he be more earnest for salvation.

"Edward Jordan and his wife are well, and desire their most affectionate love to Mr. Henry Foxall and his wife (if alive). They are very glad to hear of his welfare of body and soul: and would esteem it a singular favour to receive a letter from him soon. His brother John is gone into Wales, and does exceeding well both in spirituals and temporals. He still continues to receive the preachers. His brother Benjamin (at the Wrenn's nest) has a concern for his soul and earnestly wishes to get the preachers to his house.

"James Stokes is very poorly indeed. He has been for a year very low in mind, and past business. His mother desires that his uncle will pray for him, and that he will not fail to write.

"We have had some revival in Walsall: where our preachers meet with some kind friends. I live in Richard Longmore's house; and have lived there about twenty years.

"Elenor Rogers has been dead about a year: John is well, but not married again.

"Phebe Smith is alive and her husband; they are also old people.

"Sarah Weston has been dead some years : and her husband also.

"We are going on pretty well at Barr: the congregations are pretty good.

"Sam Barkley, our preacher who writes this, desires his most affectionate love to you and bother Whatcoat.

"I remain in dear love, your ever affectionate mother, Eliza Asbury" clxxxi.

---

clxxxi *J&L Vol III p184-185.*

15. Eliza's Death

When Eliza wrote to her son in 1800 she was 85 and described her medical problems. A modern physician specialising in elderly medicine analysed the letter. He was asked what the letter indicated about her illness, whether malnutrition or poor diet was a significant factor and whether the dependence on others to write was due to medical problems or lack of skills. He responded:

"The symptoms of leg and foot swelling in someone of 85 would be most likely caused by heart failure. Feeling sick and faint could have been associated with a myocardial infarction (or heart failure) although this is clearly only speculative. Heart failure can improve spontaneously and people do gather strength following a heart attack. Effective diuretic were not available, as far as I am aware in the 1800's.

"A heart attack would also leave her a little weaker than prior to "the afflictions". A recovery period of three to four weeks would be plausible. One could not exclude a chest infection causing heart strain or a pulmonary embolus also causing heart strain as being the causes for her episode of poor health. The fact that she died two years after this event also fits quite well as that is roughly the prognosis for these patients.

"Malnourishment can cause leg selling but this is usually caused by severe gastrointestinal disease. Other symptoms should have been prominent. I have not seen poor food intake cause significant swelling in elderly patients.

"The most likely reason for this lady being unable to write at the age of 85 was that she had poor eyesight. Glaucoma, cataracts and age related macular degeneration would all be common in this group. There are obviously a multitude of other possible reasons why she could not write, some other common ones being a stroke, Parkinson's disease or essential tremor…These comments are somewhat speculative and that other opinions may possibly come to alternative conclusions" [clxxxii].

Eliza passed away in January 1802. Her body like that of her husband was laid out by local women led by a Mrs Hodgetts [clxxxiii] and buried in St Margaret's churchyard, Great Barr on 29 January, one of three burials recorded that day. Samuel Bradbourn, later a President of the Methodist Conference, preached.

Her son didn't hear the news until 5 April and it may be that it came in a batch of letters from the President of the British Methodist Conference [clxxxiv].

Asbury says fondly on hearing of her death:

[clxxxii] *Letter to author from Dr R.A. Shinton MA MSc MD FRCP, Consultant Physician at the Birmingham Heartlands Hospital, 21 August 2001.* [clxxxiii] *MWHSB. Vol 1 p11-12 1965.* [clxxxiv] *J&L Vol II p333.*

"...and thus a lamp was lighted up in a dark place called Great Barre, in Great Britain. She was an afflicted, yet most active woman, of quick bodily powers, and masculine understanding; nevertheless so kindly all the elements were mixed in her. Her strong mind quickly felt the subduing influences of that Christian sympathy which weeps with those who weep and rejoices with those who do rejoice.

"As a woman and a wife she was chaste modest, blameless; as a mother (above all the women in the world I claim her for my own) ardently affectionate; as a "mother in Israel" few of her sex have done more by a holy walk to live and by personal labour to support, the Gospel, and to wash the saints feet; as a friend she was generous, true, and constant" [clxxxv].

St. Margaret's, Great Barr.

More than three months later Frank was to get another account [clxxxvi] of his mother's death, probably from his cousin John Rogers. Frank noted in his journal "...I learnt that a certain Mr Emery had taken all her property" [clxxxvii].

Frank told his cousin "As to her property I never expected or desired a farthing, my only wish that it might be appropriate, as all we could spare fir between forty or fifty years had been for the support of the gospel, at the dark place of my nativity."

Frank was disappointed that John Rogers was unable to give him details of her last words or prayers, but took the opportunity in his reply to enquire after his cousin's spiritual condition and enquire after Widow Griffin and Mrs Moorhead. He points out that the only person he had to correspond with in England is Dr Coke and asks that John Rogers should write once a year [clxxxviii].

Nearly sixty years later biographer Briggs researched what happened to her property: although Frank was very generous towards his mother and father, Eliza struggled to keep her hospitable home open following the death of Joseph. Briggs thought she was unaware that her son had made contingency plans with Richard Whatcoat to care for her in the event of his own death [clxxxix]. It may be that she hadn't understood what Frank had told her about his plans.

Briggs explains that "their cottage, always neat and clean, wore from year after year, the same appearance of quiet respectability and comfort.

"For nearly half a century its principal room was used as a preaching place and as such was put in order for worship punctually at the appointed hour, a cheerful fire on

[clxxxv] *J&L Vol II p333-334.* [clxxxvi] *Probably from Eliza's cousin John Rogers to whom Frank replied on 1 August 1802 J&L Vol II p242-244.* [clxxxvii] *J&L Vol II p354.* [clxxxviii] *J&L Vol III p242 – 244. The letter is addressed to John Rogers at 161, High Street, Walsall. FA assumes that John Rogers is a member of the society at Barr, though he lives someway from the village.* [clxxxix] *Briggs p352 quoting Richard Boehm.*

the hearth in the winter evenings; and the preacher, after the service, always offered refreshment before taking his, in some cases, long and dreary walk home" [cxc].

Eliza had made a simple arrangement with her landlord, the brother of one of Frank's childhood friends: to live rent free until her death in exchange for all her property [cxci]. Thus she avoided the indignity of eviction that had befell her neighbour Widow Bromwich fifty years before, or the hospitality of the workhouse.

Briggs doesn't mention that her landlord, Mr Emery, was probably the owner or landlord of the Malt Shovel pub [cxcii].

[cxc] *Briggs p347.* [cxci] *Briggs p352.* [cxcii] *A Thomas Emery is listed as landlord of the Malt Shovel in 1834. White p200.*

16. After Eliza

Frank Asbury evidently believed that the Methodist cause in Great Barr had already opened a chapel within a few hundred yards of his old home at the time of his mother's death [cxciii]. He offered to subscribe a sum annually to support its work. It appears that the chapel had not been built by then and the Society of nineteen members led by a Robert Jefferies may have even continued to meet in the cottage.

In 1808 a little chapel was erected a couple of hundred yards up Newton Road. It was part of the Wednesbury circuit but numbers declined to 14 by 1811 when it disappeared from circuit records. In 1823 it was sold to the Congregationalists and several of their eminent preachers including Robert Dale of the Birmingham Carrs Lane church served there [cxciv].

The Methodist cause in Great Barr was revived in 1866 when the Birmingham District of the Wesleyan Methodist connexion established a trust to fund and construct a Methodist Church. The Great Barr Methodist Church opened its doors in 1868.

One hundred years later the Great Barr congregation celebrated their centenary and published a small booklet to commemorate the event. There was no mention of the congregation that had kept the lamp burning in Great Barr for so many years [cxcv].

The cottage where Eliza lived and died soon had American Methodist visitors. The first recorded was the Rev John Emory, later a Bishop who called as early as 1824. He reportedly sat in the late Joseph's chair and ate at the old table. He managed to collect twenty-five of Frank Asbury's original letters home [cxcvi].

Twelve years later in 1836 the Rev Wilbur Fisk called. He was attending the Methodist Conference which was held in Birmingham that year. He enquired of the lady who lived in the cottage if there were any letters there, she reportedly replied "Law me, I didn't know the papers were good for anything. It is a year since I emptied the old trunk and burned up the contents."

The old Methodist Chapel, Newton Road, Great Barr, built in 1808 almost opposite the old Malt Shovel public house.

cxciii J&L Vol II p334. *cxciv* PWHS Ibid p102. (Sheldon article). *cxcv* Great Barr Methodist Church, 1968. *cxcvi* Wakeley p454.

Fisk acquired a two handled earthen cup which he believed the Asburys and the visiting itinerant ministers would have used and took it back to America. He then went on to the Sneal's Green school where he met Mrs Moseley, the wife of the schoolmaster, who's father was a cousin of Frank and exchanged letters with him, probably John Rogers [cxcvii]. Fisk managed to get two letters.

Fisk's guide during this visit was the local historian Joseph Reeves, "a labouring man, but quite an antiquarian in his way, who seemed to know everything connected with the neighbourhood, either in the past or present generation".

Reeves showed Fisk other sites of interest to a visiting American Methodist at that time including the grave and monument to Henry Foxall, Mayor of Georgetown in Washington DC.

They also saw the house of John Griffin who was one of those believed to have taken Frank on as an apprentice. (Other sources say that this was just 40 or so yards from the Asbury's cottage.) By 1836 a man named Thorp had moved into the house and an outraged Fisk comments "and a wretched fellow he is; it seemed a sort of sacrilege to see the house where Asbury used to live converted into a den of thieves."

John Emory (above) and Wilbur Fisk (below) were the first American visitors to the cottage.

Fisk's other comments about the neighbourhood suggest that it was still the "darke place" remembered by Frank Asbury: "The villages are full of shops for strong drink, and the streets are full of children, growing up to drink and die, as their fathers now drink and die before them; and yet, who cares for their souls" [cxcviii].

In 1885 the Wesleyan Methodist Conference, encouraged by the biographer Frederick Briggs, who had gained funds in America, built a chapel on Birmingham's Soho Road close to the site of

[cxcvii] *J&L Vol III p242-246.* [cxcviii] *Fisk p605 - 609.*

Manwoods where Frank is reputed to have preached his first sermon and named it the Asbury Memorial Church cxcix. The building, though no longer part of the mainstream British Methodist Connexion, now provides a home for the Caribbean based Wesleyan Holiness Church.

The cottage continued to receive interest and attention from Methodists throughout the world. W.C. Sheldon contributed an article for the Proceedings of the Wesleyan Historical Society on the landmarks of Asbury's youth. This was reprinted as a booklet for visitors to the area cc.

Local historians commented on the cottage's significance and soon after the Second World War new legislation enabled West Bromwich Borough Council, then the appropriate local authority, to apply for the building to be "listed" as having especial historical interest and thereby protected from future demolition or damaging alteration.

In January 1950 the International Methodist Historical Society wrote to West Bromwich council reiterating the importance of the cottage as the most important Methodist historical site in the Black Country. The Society suggested that should the cottage be for sale, it might be bought, restored and furnished.

Ownership of the cottage had passed, along with the adjoining Malt Shovel Cottage, the malt house and Malt Shovel public house, to the Darby Brewery Ltd, although by then the cottage did not conform to modern housing standards. In 1955 the two cottages were transferred to council ownership.

The cottage was still occupied by a Mrs Randles and her family who, we are told by the Town Clerk of West Bromwich at the time, "deserve the highest praise for the understanding way in which, over many years, they had been prepared to receive visitors into their home, often at times when it must have been quite inconvenient for viewing. Many tributes have been received by Mrs Randles from American visitors who have had the opportunity of seeing this historic place."

Mrs Randles was found alternative accommodation locally in 1957, although it is believed that a Mrs Searle also lived in the cottage for a short time. Plans were drawn up to refurbish the cottage using Thomas Rayson, the same architect who had recently assisted in the restoration of the Old Rectory, childhood home of the Wesleys in Epworth, Lincolnshire.

The basic features of the cottage were restored, particularly the inglenook fireplace which was known to exist behind the modern kitchen range which had served the Randles. At the same time the council restored the adjoining Malt Shovel Cottage to modern housing standards and surrounding gardens. The intention was for the occupier of the Malt Shovel Cottage to assist with the upkeep of the site.

---

cxcix *Hackwood "Handsworth" 2001.* cc *PWHS Ibid.*

West Bromwich Council clearly hoped that the visitors to cottage would also visit other local sites including the 13th century Manor House in Wednesbury and the 16th century Oak House in West Bromwich, where John Wesley himself preached.

A commemorative plaque records:

THIS COTTAGE
NOW THE PROPERTY OF THE
COUNTY BOROUGH OF WEST BROMWICH
WAS THE BOYHOOD HOME OF
FRANCIS ASBURY
(1745 – 1816)
"THE PROPHET OF THE LONG ROAD"
WHO WAS SENT TO AMERICA BY JOHN WESLEY IN 1771
AND BECAME THE FIRST BISHOP OF THE
AMERICAN METHODIST CHURCH
DEDICATED TO PERPETUAL REMEMBRANCE
IN ASSOCIATION WITH THE WORLD METHODIST COUNCIL
AFTER RESTORATION 27TH NOVEMBER 1959 [cci]

However shortly afterwards, in the early 1960s, Newton Road was widened to become a dual carriageway with the malt house, public house and adjoining Malt House Cottage demolished. This left the Asbury Cottage next to the new road on an artificial knoll.

American visitors to the site were not always impressed by what they found. In 1970 the Wolverhampton Express and Star published an article headed "Shrine Shocks Americans". The visitors were drawn from Washington and Baltimore and had visited Epworth the previous day "What a let down", said the leader of the party "I would have thought the local Methodists would have taken the trouble to maintain the cottage as Bishop Asbury had lived there".

The local branch of the Wesleyan Historical Society was urged to help the local council improve the facilities [ccii].

The cottage now has an exhibition of Frank Asbury's life together with

Cottage Plaque.

[cci] *JM Day, PWHS, 1959 p83-85.* [ccii] *MWHSB 1970 p10.*

pictures and furniture from the period. It is open just two days a year, but can be opened by special request for visiting parties.

When writing to Eliza after the death of his father in 1798 Frank had asked his mother to spend a few guineas on a "perfect plain portrait of yourself" [cciii]. Sometime before her death she complied with his request and given the state of her health it was probably painted at the cottage. The portrait is 16 x 18 inches but the artist is unknown.

In 1805 Frank gave the picture to his friend George Suckley of New York who had visited the cottage on a number of occasions. The portrait stayed in the ownership of the Suckley family until 1954 when it was given to Drew University [cciv].

In 2002 a framed copy of the portrait Eliza had painted for her son was presented for display in the cottage.

Eliza was home.

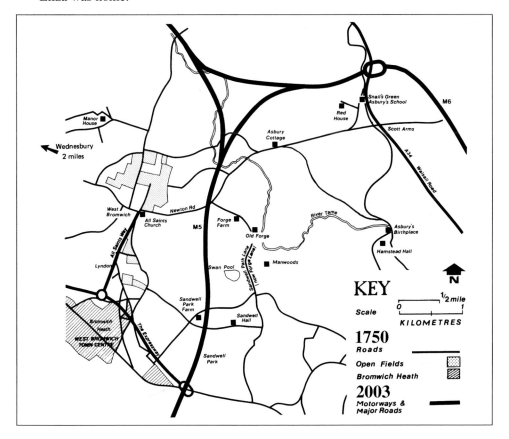

West Bromwich in Eliza's time with today's major roads superimposed.

[cciii] *J&L Vol III p170.* [cciv] *Dr. K Rowe, Drew University, email 25 September 2001.*

Afterword

This small book has taken many hours of work over about a period of three years. It may be obvious to the reader that I share many of the religious views of both Eliza and Frank Asbury.

Both contributed to the development of Methodism in dramatically different ways:

Eliza stayed at home in that little cottage. Despite her bereavement at losing Sarah in childhood and Frank to America, week in and week out, for half a century, she opened her home for worship. Doubtless she took on the many problems of the people who come seeking help at any church in any time. It is by no means certain that her husband entirely shared her enthusiasm and there remain many question marks about his behaviour.

Frank began a long journey which meant that by the time he died, in 1816, he had probably seen more of the emerging United States than any other individual. Countless times in his journal he recorded both the highs and lows of his long witness. He was not always welcome and frequently knew discouragement and opposition.

Eliza and Frank would probably be surprised to know that by today's standards both are seen as extraordinary.

The strength of Methodism as an expression of Christian faith is that it stresses commitment and consistency. Frank travelled and Elizabeth stayed where she was, there could be no greater contrast in the way they expressed their commitment. However when both were convinced that this was God's will for their lives, they were consistent in fulfilling that belief.

Eliza and Frank were very ordinary, working class people from the West Midlands. However they, and their fellow Methodists, were able to take their vision of a loving God and a wonderful Saviour, so seriously that they sought to change the world.

Bibliography

Asbury, F. "The Journal and Letters of Francis Asbury". Published Jointly by the Epworth Press, London and the Abingdon Press, Nashville, 1958, 1st edn 1821.

Asbury, H. "A Methodist Saint" New York, 1927.

Baker, F. "John Wesley and the Church of England" Epworth, Peterborough 1999.

Bebbington, B.V. "Evangelicalism in Modern Britain", Routledge, London, 1989, 1999 edn.

Bond, John Wesley, Anecdotes of Bishop Asbury, handwritten MS 1817.

Briggs Rev M.A "Bishop Asbury: A biographical study" Wesleyan Conference Office, London 1879.

(BMWHS) Bulletin of the Midlands Wesleyan Historical Society 1965-1982.

Court W.H.B. "The Rise of Midlands Industries 1600-1838, Oxford, 1938.

Rupert E. Davies "Methodism" Epworth 1963.

Duren, L. Francis Asbury, Founder of American Methodism and Unofficial Minister of State, MacMillan, New York, 1928.

Dilworth, D "The Tame Mills of Staffordshire" Phillimore, London & Chichester. 1976.

Donovan, Jane unpublished emails, researching the life of Henry Foxall, Georgetown UMC, Washington DC, January 2003.

Ede, J.F. "History of Wednesbury" Simmons Publishing, Wednesbury 1962, 1991 Ed.

Fisk, Wilbur " Travels in Europe through England, Ireland, Scotland, Italy Germany and the Netherlands", New York 1838.

Gentry, P.W. "Francis Asbury – the Wesley of America" Moorley's Derby 1996.

Great Barr Methodist Church, "The Story of a Century 1868-1968" 1968.

Griffith, George "The Free Schools and Endowments of Staffordshire". Whittaker & Co. 1860.

Hackwood, F.W. "Handsworth Old and New", reprinted by Brewin Books 2001.

Hackwood, F.W. "History of West Bromwich", 1895, reprinted by Brewin Books 2001.

Hartill, Rev Percy "The Story of All Saints' Parish Church West Bromwich" British Publishing Company, Gloucester 1925.

Hopkins, Eric "Birmingham – the first manufacturing town in the World 1760-1840", Weidenfeld and Nicolson, London, 1989.

Hutton, William "An History of Birmingham" 1783. Republished by EP Publishing 1976.

"Hymns and Psalms" Methodist Publishing House, 1983.

Lewis, J. Francis Asbury, Epworth, London, 1927.

Martin, J.M. The Growth of Population in Warwickshire in the 18th Century. Dugdale Occasional Papers Series 23 1976.

Parker, Michael St John "Life in Georgian Britain", Pitkin, 2000.

Prince, H.H., "The Romance of Early Methodism In and Around Wednesbury etc," West Bromwich, 1925.

Reeves, Joseph unpublished and lost MS "A History of the Rise and Progress of the Wesleyan Methodists in Birmingham, Wednesbury, Dudley, West Bromwich and Its Vicinity; 1742 - 1842" extracts quoted in Hackwood, Wilkinson, Prince, MWHS, etc. This is a major source of information, but only extracts have ever been published. It was last quoted by E.Lissimore in 1965.

(PWHS) Proceedings of the Wesley Historical Society.

Stacey, John "Groundwork of Theology" John Stacey, Epworth Press (Revised edn 1984).

Sheldon, W.C "Early Methodism in Hill and its Neighbourhood, Birmingham" Buckler and Webb, 1903.

Skipp, V. "Discovering Sheldon (1960)", "Discovering Bickenhill (1963)" University of Birmingham Dept of Extra Mural Studies.

Strickland, W.P. "The Pioneer Bishop" Wesleyan Conference Office, London, 1858.

Telford, John "The Methodist Hymn Book Illustrated" Epworth 1934.

Thompson, E.P. "The Making of the English Working Class" Penguin, London, 1991.

Vickers, J.A. "Francis Asbury" Foundery Press, Peterborough 1993.

Wakeley, W "The Mother of Bishop Asbury" The Ladies Repository August 1867.

Wesley, J "A Plain Account of the People Called Methodists" reprint of eighth edition 1786 by The John Marcon Press.

White, William "History, Gazetteer and Directory of Staffordshire" Sheffield 1834.

Wigger, J.H. "Taking Heaven By Storm" Illinois 1998.

Wilkinson, W.J. "The History of Methodism in the Wednesbury Circuit", Darlaston 1895.

Woodall, Richard "The Barr Story" Tector, Aldridge, undated but believed to be early 50s.

Index